MW01257794

A Gentle Introduction to Old English

A Gentle Introduction to Old English

◆

Murray McGillivray

broadview press

© 2011 Murray McGillivray

All rights reserved. The use of any part of this publication reproduced, transmitted in any form or by any means, electronic, mechanical, photocopying, recording, or otherwise, or stored in a retrieval system, without prior written consent of the publisher—or in the case of photocopying, a licence from Access Copyright (Canadian Copyright Licensing Agency), One Yonge Street, Suite 1900, Toronto, Ontario M5E 1E5—is an infringement of the copyright law.

Library and Archives Canada Cataloguing in Publication

McGillivray, Murray, 1953-
    A gentle introduction to Old English / Murray McGillivray.

Includes bibliographical references and index.
ISBN 978-1-55111-841-3

    1. English language—Old English, ca. 450-1100—Grammar—Textbooks.
2. English language—Old English, ca. 450-1100—Textbooks.   3. English language—
Old English, ca. 450-1100—Texts.   I. Title.

PE124.M35 2010   429'.82421   C2010-905964-6

Broadview Press is an independent, international publishing house, incorporated in 1985.

We welcome comments and suggestions regarding any aspect of our publications—please feel free to contact us at the addresses below or at broadview@broadviewpress.com.

North America
Post Office Box 1243, Peterborough, Ontario, Canada K9J 7H5
2215 Kenmore Avenue, Buffalo, NY, USA 14207
Tel: (705) 743-8990; Fax: (705) 743-8353
email: customerservice@broadviewpress.com

UK, Europe, Central Asia, Middle East, Africa, India, and Southeast Asia
Eurospan Group, 3 Henrietta St., London WC2E 8LU, United Kingdom
Tel: 44 (0) 1767 604972; Fax: 44 (0) 1767 601640
email: eurospan@turpin-distribution.com

Australia and New Zealand
NewSouth Books
c/o TL Distribution, 15-23 Helles Ave., Moorebank, NSW, Australia 2170
Tel: (02) 8778 9999; Fax: (02) 8778 9944
email: orders@tldistribution.com.au

www.broadviewpress.com

Broadview Press acknowledges the financial support of the Government of Canada through the Canada Book Fund for our publishing activities.

This book is printed on paper containing 100% post-consumer fibre.

Edited by Martin Boyne

Typesetting and assembly: True to Type Inc., Claremont, Canada.

PRINTED IN CANADA

Contents

◆

Preface • 7
Introduction • 11

Chapter 1: Some Grammatical Terminology You Will Need • 13
Chapter 2: Pronunciation and Spelling of Old English • 23
Chapter 3: Strong Nouns and an Introduction to Old English Cases • 30
Chapter 4: Demonstratives; Nominative and Genitive Cases • 36
Chapter 5: A Few Old English Verbs; Accusative and Dative Cases • 42
Chapter 6: Weak Verbs: Subjunctive, Participles, Infinitives • 50
Chapter 7: Strong Nouns and Cases • 58
Chapter 8: Strong Verbs; Personal Pronouns • 65
Chapter 9: Weak Nouns and Noun Oddities; Numerals • 71
Chapter 10: Adjectives • 78
Chapter 11: Word Order in Noun Phrases and Sentences;
             the Subjunctive • 85
Chapter 12: Old English Metre, Poetic Diction, and Poetic Syntax • 92

Prose Readings
    Abraham and Isaac • 101
    The Birth of Jesus • 117
    The Story of Ohthere • 127
    Aelfric's *Colloquy* • 151

Select Bibliography • 199
Index • 201

Preface

◆

This textbook is designed for the average contemporary student of Old English.

Such a person does not exist, of course. Each student is an individual, with individual interests, aversions, strengths, and weaknesses. Nevertheless, I think it is possible to draw a reasonable police sketch or composite portrait of the "average student" based on characteristics shared by large numbers of early twenty-first-century students who enroll in Old English courses or who try to learn Old English on their own.

The average student these days does not come to Old English with a firm foundation of grammatical terminology or skill in grammatical analysis. This person is unlikely to have studied grammar in school, and if she or he speaks more than one language, that is very unlikely to be the result of any kind of formal language training.

The average student, on the other hand, can quickly develop real fascination with Anglo-Saxon writings and culture, both because of the strong sense of estrangement and cultural and historical difference those writings create and because many things in that strange world are eerily familiar, whether from gaming environments, Hollywood film, or just the normal persistence in our culture of structures, relationships, and ways of thought with very ancient origins.

Standing in the way of that potential for genuine engagement has often been the sheer difficulty of the Old English language, a challenge even for students with more grammatical knowledge than average when the language is presented as a series of memorization tasks divorced from any obvious immediate application.

The traditional method of teaching Old English has aimed, I think laudably, at giving the student comprehensive understanding of the structures of the language. This textbook aims instead to give students access to Old English texts

7

as soon as possible, on the theory that, for the average current student, the excitement of actually reading and understanding these ancient documents is more likely to inspire curiosity about the specifics of the language they are written in than comprehensive knowledge of the rules of grammar is to spark any kind of passion. For this reason, no attempt is made to "cover" the grammar of Old English, but rather to give students a basic understanding of the most common structures, just enough to get by on when reading texts, and some sense of what kinds of variation there are.

With its companion website, which does provide a reasonably full grammar, *A Gentle Introduction* also draws on the strong media literacy of the average contemporary student of Old English, by providing some support and some room for exploration beyond the bounds of the printed book. The average student these days, whether enrolled in an undergraduate or graduate Old English course or not, is a self-directed learner, used to calling on a variety of media in a variety of life-contexts and on a variety of devices for information and instruction. The companion website allows students to access the course materials where they are and learn when they want to.

Many of the concepts that have guided the development of this book are not new at all but have been grasped intuitively or arrived at experimentally by generations of teachers. I want particularly to acknowledge the contribution to my pedagogical thinking of my own first teacher of the language, Martin Puhvel, whose terrifying first assignment for us was to come back the next week prepared to translate from Old English without notes the opening of the story of Ohthere (and to memorize a declension, of course). Martin strongly believed that if he could get us reading the texts, he could hook us on the language. In my case, he certainly succeeded.

I also want to acknowledge the inspiration of textbooks in other early languages, particularly Wheelock's Latin and the Viking Society Old Norse textbooks, both of which have provided admirable models for some aspects of this current book. As well, early experiments of Anglo-Saxonists with programmed Old English instruction, particularly the computer-based lessons developed by Constance Hieatt and O.D. Macrae-Gibson, were an inspiration at the beginning.

Finally, I want to thank all of my students in Old English classes over the years and acknowledge their contribution, with special thanks to the students who suffered through a trial run of this book in 2008-09 and those who from 1996 to 2009 helped me to conceive and improve the online materials that became the companion website. (Robin Norris of Carleton University also pioneered this text in her course pre-publication and gave valuable feedback.)

I certainly will never forget those few outstanding students of mine who easily grasped the rules of Old English, and some of whom went on to further study and even professional careers in the subject, but the warmest place in my heart is actually for students who struggled a little, who were a bit turned off by the subject matter, who overcame their difficulties with my course only gradually if at all, but who persisted and in doing so taught me what little I know about how to present this material for the average learner.

This book is dedicated to the reader it is conceived for: the average student of Old English.

Introduction

◆

As the title of this volume indicates, its primary aim is to ease the way of the beginner to competent reading knowledge of the Old English language. Rather than attempting to present a full account of the grammar of the language, this introductory text concentrates on those features of the language that will be encountered most frequently in the course of an introductory Old English class taken over one or two semesters, and especially on those aspects of the language that must be thoroughly understood for basic reading knowledge. As a result of this emphasis on basic competence, some features of the language are given greater prominence than in traditional textbooks, and other features that are seldom encountered are simply not addressed. More advanced students, and those whose interest is primarily linguistic rather than literary or historical, may find profit later on in a more comprehensive introductory text, such as that by Mitchell and Robinson, and will eventually need to consult one or more of the comprehensive grammars (Campbell, Sievers-Brunner, Mitchell's *Syntax*, and the soon-to-be published Hogg).

I try to make as few assumptions as I can about the grammatical and linguistic preparation that students may have for the study of Old English. Basic English grammar is seldom taught, or at least seldom taught thoroughly, in schools these days, and fewer students than in the past have formal training in a second language or especially a classical language. The text begins for that reason with a chapter introducing most of the basic grammatical terminology required for the study of Old English (although some concepts are introduced in later chapters as needed). I have discovered in my own classroom that even students who claim a knowledge of words such as noun, adjective, and verb may need a refresher before applying them confidently to modern English, let alone venturing into the choppier waters of an earlier stage of English. As for abstruse concepts such as the prepositional phrase or the relative pronoun, the safest assumption is that undergraduate students and many graduate students will need to learn them at the beginning of their Old English course.

When specifically Old English grammatical concepts and patterns are introduced in the subsequent chapters, they are brought in gently and often gradually in order not to overwhelm the beginner with terminology and grammatical memorization, and the student is given an opportunity through exercises to see how each newly introduced feature operates in the language. Examples given in the chapters are drawn as far as possible from actual Old English texts that have survived in manuscript, though particularly in the earlier chapters the cited sentences are often simplified by elimination of material irrelevant to the point being illustrated. The practice exercises, on the other hand, most often involve either the interpretation or the production of "manufactured" Old English—that is, Old English not drawn directly from original texts. This allows a restricted subset of Old English vocabulary to be used so that the student can focus on the grammatical concept being taught rather than on new vocabulary. Active production of Old English sentences, an instructional method widely used by teachers of classical languages, allows the student to develop a feel for how a particular grammatical feature makes meaning in the language.

Simple reading texts are introduced as early as practicable. All are drawn from actual Old English sources, but in the earlier chapters the sentence structure is often simplified and the text edited to focus on the grammatical concepts that have been recently introduced. Four prose texts that have not been simplified or edited for brevity and grammatical focus are included at the back of the book: two short biblical excerpts (the story of the sacrifice of Isaac and the story of the birth of Jesus), each with on-the-page glosses and explanatory notes; and two more substantial texts (the story of Ohthere and Aelfric's *Colloquy*), each followed by its own full glossary.

This textbook is best used in conjunction with its companion website (http://www.OEGrammar.ca), where a wide variety of additional resources are made available for the learner, including pronunciation samples, additional interactive exercises, and online versions of the reading texts where each word can be clicked on in turn to get the corresponding glossary entry. Additional online texts, both prose and poetry, that are not included in this book but that could be used as additional reading in a one-semester Old English course or to extend the course to a second semester are provided on the *Old English Reader* companion website (http://www.OEReader.ca).

Although this textbook is designed primarily for students following a formal classroom or online course in Old English, it is also perfectly suitable for students learning the language on their own without a teacher. Self-taught students are best advised to proceed slowly enough through the material that they are certain they have grasped each point before moving on to a new one, and to attempt all of the available exercises (in print or online).

Chapter 1
Some Grammatical Terminology You Will Need

◆

Learning Old English, even in a beginners' course, will require you to develop an understanding of the grammar of the language. Luckily, there are only a few instances in which Old English has grammatical structures that do not exist at all in modern English. So if you understand modern English grammar, you have a solid head start on Old English.

However, many students today, however fluent they may be in English, do not necessarily have a strong grasp of grammatical terminology as it applies to English. They know how to speak and write correctly, but not how to name parts of sentences analytically. Learning grammatical terminology for modern English will help you to understand and identify grammatical structures in Old English, so this introductory chapter provides a brief outline of grammar using modern English examples. Even if you feel you have a very good grasp of grammatical terminology, it might be a good idea to review it by reading this chapter before beginning to work with the following chapters of this text-book.

Parts of Speech

The words of English (and of Old English) can be divided into classes of words that have different grammatical functions. These are called the "parts of speech." It is important to identify the part of speech of any particular word in order to understand its function in a sentence. Fluent speakers of English do this automatically, but you may well need to become quite conscious about it in reading Old English. Note that the part of speech cannot always be determined by knowing what the word is, since some words can serve as different parts of speech depending on the various roles they can play in a sentence:

I **love** your new hat. (verb)
Love will keep us together. (noun)

That's my friend Robin. (pronoun)
I love **that** new hat. (adjective)
It is unfortunate **that** you did not check with the manager.
    (conjunction)

Nouns

A *noun* is any word that names a person, place, thing, idea, animal, quality, or activity.

person: **teacher**
place: **park**
thing: **chair**
idea: **togetherness**
animal: **beaver**
quality: **height**
activity: **riding**

Notice that not all nouns refer to concrete things—some refer to abstract ideas.

Two tests to see if a word is a noun are whether you can put an *article* (such as **the** or **a**) or a *possessive* (like **his**) in front of the word and make a complete unit ("his hat"; "the process"); and whether the word can be the *subject* of a sentence (see *Parts of a Sentence* below).

Names of specific people, animals, or places are called *proper nouns*; they are capitalized in modern English. Proper nouns usually satisfy only the second of the two tests just mentioned:

Barack Obama
New York
the planet **Jupiter**

A *noun phrase* consists of a noun and all its modifiers, including such things as articles and adjectives:

the 44th **President** of the United States
the Big **Apple**
my beautiful **laundrette**
the **fat** woman next door

Pronouns

A *pronoun* is a word that stands in for a noun that has been previously mentioned or that is known from the context; a pronoun may also stand in for an unknown noun:

> When Bob gets here, **he**'s going to be in trouble!
> **You**'re looking pretty self-satisfied today.
> **Someone** took my calculator!

Some common types of pronoun are *personal pronouns* (words like **I**, **she**, **they**, **we**) that refer to people or things; *demonstrative pronouns* ("I don't like **that**"; "**this** is my size") that are the linguistic equivalent of pointing to something; *interrogative pronouns* ("**who** loves you, baby?"; "**what** do you think of that?") that are used to ask questions; *indefinite pronouns* (words like **anyone**, **each**, **some**) that refer to unknown nouns; and *relative pronouns* such as **who**, **which**, **that**, often used to connect two sentences (so that "The man is wearing the red sweater" plus "The man is my dad" can become "The man **who** is wearing the red sweater is my dad").

When a pronoun stands in for a noun that either has already been mentioned or is inferred from the context, that noun is called the pronoun's *antecedent*. So in the sentence "When Bob gets here, he's going to be in trouble," the proper noun **Bob** is the antecedent of the pronoun **he**, since they both refer to the same person.

Articles

English has two *articles*, a *definite article* **the** and an *indefinite article* **a** or **an**. Articles precede nouns (and any adjectives modifying the nouns) and indicate whether the reference is to a specific individual (or group) or to one that is indefinite or unknown:

the dogs
an ancient map
the weather
a snowstorm

Verbs

A *verb* tells us something about the *subject* of a *sentence*. It expresses action, state, or relationship. The subject of a sentence is the noun or noun phrase the sentence is about; the verb typically begins the part of the sentence called the *predicate*, which most usually asserts something about the subject:

The brown dog **ran** away.
(Here, the subject is "the brown dog"; the predicate is "ran away"; and the verb is "ran.")
This purse **feels** extremely heavy.
(Subject "this purse"; predicate "feels extremely heavy"; verb "feels.")
Three trains **are arriving** at 3:10.
(Subject "three trains"; predicate "are arriving at 3:10"; verb "are arriving.")
Your kettle **is boiling**.
(Subject "your kettle"; predicate "is boiling"; verb "is boiling.")

Verbs can be *simple* (composed of one word like "ran" and "feels") or *compound* (composed of more than one word like "are arriving" and "is boiling"). They may change their form to signify *tense* (which designates the time of the action of the verb: "had felt sad"; "disappeared"; "is running"; "sank"; "will conquer"). They also express *mood* (the most common are *indicative mood*, which is used in most sentences, and *imperative mood*, used to give commands—"**Drop** dead, loser" [imperative] versus "The loser **drops** dead" [indicative]). And in present tense they have differing forms depending on *number* and *person* (plural "They **run**" compared to first-person singular "I **run**" and third-person singular "He **runs**"). We call a pronoun and its verb *first person* if it refers to or includes the person speaking (**I, we**), *second person* if it refers to or includes the person being spoken to (**you**), and *third person* if it refers to neither the speaker nor the person being spoken to (**he, she, it, they**).

Adjectives

An *adjective* describes, identifies, or quantifies a noun or pronoun and is said to "modify" the noun it relates to. Adjectives usually, but not always, precede the noun they modify:

> my **paternal** uncle
> a **freak** accident
> her **astonishing** collection of hats
> **negative** energy
> Her collection of hats is **astonishing**.
> The energy in the room felt entirely **negative** to me.

Adverbs

An *adverb* specifies such things as time, place, manner, degree, or cause, and can modify a verb, an adjective, another adverb, or even an entire sentence. One common method of forming adverbs is to add the suffix "-ly" to an adjective—so that "thrifty" becomes "thriftily"—but there are many adverbs that do not end in "ly":

> I live **here**, in the green house.
> I was expecting it **sooner**.
> **Slowly** she unpacked the **carefully** wrapped package but **then very suddenly** burst into tears.

Prepositions

The function of a *preposition* is to make a prepositional phrase out of a noun or noun phrase, which then can function as a kind of adverb or adjective in a sentence. A *prepositional phrase* consists of the preposition and the noun or noun phrase, called the *object of the preposition*. Prepositions are usually short single words, although there are a few consisting of more than one word:

> **under** my hat
> **on** the lam
> **out of** Africa
> **after** the gold rush

Conjunctions

Conjunctions act to join things together, including words and phrases. Sentences can also be attached to each other using conjunctions, resulting in a longer sentence with more than one *clause* (the sentences that were combined). If the clauses in the resulting sentence are of equal importance, the conjunction is a *coordinating conjunction*; if one is more important than the other, the conjunction is a *subordinating conjunction*:

> I'm going east **and** you're going west.
> I'm going east **or** I'm going west.
> (Here, the ideas are of equal importance, so both **and** and **or** are
>   coordinating conjunctions.)
> **Before** you go west, I'm going east.
> (Here "I'm going east" is the main idea, and "before you go west" acts
>   as an adverb by specifying the time when "I'm going east," so
>   **before** is a subordinating conjunction.)

The clause introduced by a subordinating conjunction is called a *subordinate clause*; the clause to which it is subordinated is called the *main clause*.

Note that a sequence of words must include both a verb and its subject (see below) to form a clause; sequences that do not have a verb and its subject can at most be called *phrases*.

Parts of a Sentence

Subject and Predicate

A sentence or clause is composed of a *subject* and a *predicate*. The subject is almost always the topic of the sentence in English (what the sentence is about). It can be a noun or *noun phrase* (which most frequently consists of a noun and its modifiers or a pronoun). The predicate includes a verb and asserts or asks something about the subject. In modern English, the subject almost always comes at the beginning of the sentence, with the predicate afterwards; this is not always the case in Old English. In the following examples, the subject is bolded and the predicate is in italics:

Life *sucks.*

Alfred the Great, the King of the West Saxons, *received the*
  allegiance of Gudrum after defeating him at the battle of Wedmore.

Do **androids** *dream of electric sheep?*

Verbs and Objects

Not all verbs take *objects*, but the large number of verbs that do are called
transitive verbs. An object is a noun or noun phrase (although pronouns and
other noun-like things can also fill that role) that "receives the action" of the
verb:

> The early morning sun illuminated **the tree-tops**.
> He despises **pettiness** and abhors **small-talk**.
> They hit **the open road**.

Not everything in the part of a sentence after its main verb is necessarily an
object. For example, *linking verbs*, those that in some way assert identity,
connect a subject with a *subject complement*, either another noun phrase or a
predicate adjective, rather than transferring an action to an object:

> Mary was **disconsolate**.
> Barack Obama became **the 44th President of the United States** on
>   January 20, 2009.

Some verbs, those involving giving or telling (or similar concepts), can take
two objects:

> I gave *the dog* **a bone**.
> I told *my son* **a bedtime story**.
> I made *my wife* **a cake**.

One of the objects is called the *direct object*, the other the *indirect object*. The
direct object directly receives the action of the verb (**the bone** is what was
given, **the story** what was told, **the cake** what was made). The indirect object,
in italics in the examples above, is a kind of beneficiary of the action of the

verb, but not a direct recipient. The indirect object comes first in modern English (although not necessarily in Old English). To tell which is the direct object and which is the indirect object, try rephrasing using the prepositions **to** or **for**: the object that takes the preposition is the indirect object in the original sentence:

> I gave a bone *to* **the dog**.
> I made a cake *for* **my wife**.

Changes in the Form of Words

Inflections

Old English is an *inflected language*, which means that it communicates a fair bit of its meaning by changes in the form of words. Modern English is much less inflected because of changes and simplifications that happened during a period of about five hundred years after the Norman Conquest of 1066, although a few inflections do remain in the modern language. For example, we change the form of the verb **run** to put it in the past tense as **ran** (change of vowel), and we change the form of the word **dog** to make it plural (**dogs**) or to make it possessive (**dog's**). These changes to the forms of words are called *inflections* in general; patterns of changes that affect nouns and pronouns (and adjectives in Old English) are called *declensions*, and those that affect verbs are called *conjugations*.

Declensions and Cases

Cases are changes in the form of nouns and noun-like words that indicate the role of the word in the sentence. Modern English has only two cases for nouns: a general case and a *possessive* case, which is used to indicate ownership and similar relationships:

	general case	*possessive case*
singular	the dog	the dog's bone
plural	the dogs	the dogs' bones

Things get a little more complex for personal pronouns, where a subjective case, an objective case, and a possessive case can be seen. For example, we say "**He** loves **me**," but we say "**I** love **him**," *not* "**Me** loves **he**."

These changes of form help to indicate sentence role, specifically distinguishing between subject and object. **Me** and **him** are in the *objective case* in modern English. **I** and **he** are in the *subjective case*. (The corresponding possessive-case forms are **my** and **his**.) Old English has one further commonly used case that modern English does not have, so almost all nouns, adjectives, and pronouns change their forms to indicate four different classes of sentence roles. In addition, they can change form to indicate number, that is, whether a noun or noun-like word is singular or plural.

Conjugations

There are two main classes of modern English verbs: *regular verbs* and *irregular verbs*. Regular verbs add "-ed" to make the past tense; irregular verbs change their vowel to make the past tense:

> I **knock** on the door.
> I **knocked** on the door.
> I **run** from the room.
> I **ran** from the room.

Most of the verbs that are considered irregular in modern English descend from the class of verbs called *strong verbs* in Old English. There were many more of them, and far from being irregular they followed definite rules. The general situation was similar to the predictable groups of irregular verbs in modern English, where if you know the pattern, you can figure out how another verb will be formed that works in the same way:

> I **sw***i***m** every day.
> I **sw***a***m** yesterday.
> I told my dad I had **sw***u***m**.
> (And, similarly, *begin, began, begun; sing, sang, sung; ring, rang, rung*.)

EXERCISE 1A:
Take a sentence or two from a newspaper or website. Divide a page in your notebook into columns for parts of speech (nouns, adjectives, verbs, adverbs,

articles, prepositions, conjunctions), and then put each word in your sentence into the proper column.

Identify the sentence role (subject, direct object, indirect object, object of a preposition) of each of the bolded noun phrases:
1. My mum made **my dad** a cake for **his birthday** but she forgot **the flour**.
2. **Our neighbours** are very peculiar people and **we** think they must be artists.
3. We don't get **many visitors** here at all, actually.
4. When **Julia** saw how big it was, she got **the turkey platter** from **the cupboard**.
5. The milk is over there beside **the sink**, if you wouldn't mind bringing **my mother** a glass.

For the bolded words in each of the following sentences, decide first whether they form a noun phrase or a clause, and then, if they do form a clause, whether they constitute a main or subordinate clause:
1. After **I finish my homework**, we can play catch outside.
2. Before **every morning's sunrise**, there's a veritable cacophony of birds outside the window.
3. The **long, cold, dry winters** and intense parched summers are slowly destroying my skin.
4. I wept to see her in such a state and **I tried to rescue her**.
5. Because **there was no barrier**, the motorcycle skidded over the edge.
6. Even though they didn't win this game, **they can still advance to the finals**.

Chapter 2
Pronunciation and Spelling of Old English

◆

The Old English Alphabet

The Old English alphabet, like the modern English alphabet, is based on the Roman letters, but the alphabet is slightly different than the one we use, as you will see if you glance at some of the readings in this text. The Anglo-Saxons did not use the letters **v** and **j** (which were incorporated into the alphabet later), and **k**, **q** and **z** were used only very occasionally. They did use the Roman letter **æ** (called "ash" in Old English), which we do not use. They also introduced three letters not present in the Roman alphabet, although one of these (wyn) is represented by a **w** in modern editions and in this text, so it need not be learned at this point. The other two letters—"thorn," which is **Þ** as a capital and **þ** as a small letter, and "eth," which is **Ð** and **ð**—were both developed by Anglo-Saxon scribes to represent a sound that was not present in Latin (and for that reason was not in the Roman alphabet), the sound that modern English represents with the letters **th**. (These two letters, thorn and eth, were for all practical purposes interchangeable.)

How do we know how Old English was pronounced?

Actually, we don't have a very accurate idea of Old English pronunciation, compared to how accurately we can describe the pronunciation of languages that are spoken now. It would probably take even the best modern phonologist of Old English some time to learn to communicate fluently with a shipload of sword-waving Anglo-Saxons who arrived through a time-tunnel at a beach in the modern world, just as it takes someone who has learned to read French entirely through books some time to make herself understood in Paris or Montréal, no matter how much Balzac she has read. Nevertheless, we do know quite a bit about how Old English was pronounced, and since the like-

like the doctor?

lihood of meeting time-travelling Anglo-Saxons is fairly remote, we can reach a standard of pronunciation that will satisfy most of the people we will need to use the language with.

The knowledge that we do have about Old English pronunciation comes from a number of different sources: the Anglo-Saxons' use of the Roman alphabet to represent sounds in their language that must in some cases have been quite different from the sounds of Latin; the forms that words from Latin and other languages take when they are adopted into Old English, and the forms that Old English words take when they are represented by Latin- or French-speaking scribes; evidence about English and its dialects from later periods; evidence from the related languages of other Germanic peoples. By combining these various different kinds of evidence, we are able to get a very good idea of what the usual pronunciation of Old English was, and some idea of pronunciations in different dialects of the language.

In this text and its accompanying website, pronunciation (to an adequate standard) of the late West Saxon dialect, which is the dialect in which most texts survive, will be taught. You will find that if you make an honest effort to acquire the proper pronunciation you will have an easier time reading (and in the case of many words even understanding) the texts.

How to Study Pronunciation

If you are using this text in connection with a class, your teacher will almost certainly give you opportunities to practise, likely by having you read texts out loud. To practise outside of the classroom, use the sound clips provided on the website. You may wish to listen to the sound clips first, and then read the explanations, or you may wish to start with the explanations and proceed to the sound clips. It's a good idea to do both, in any case, since the ear can be deceptive if you don't have an idea of what you're hearing, and since explanations cannot give a real idea of what sounds are like. When using the sound clips, listen to each several times, and try to produce pronunciations as much like what you are hearing as possible. Speak out loud if your situation permits this, since speaking out loud has been shown to improve auditory memory.

Pronunciation of Consonant Sounds

1) (This is the easy part. Enjoy.)
The following consonants are pronounced in Old English in much the same way as they are in modern English:

b, d, k, l, m, n, p, r, t, x
·(The letter **r** may well have represented a "rolled" or trilled sound as in
Scots, so do trill it if you can.)

2) The consonants **s**, **f**, and **þ** / **ð** behave in similar ways and are pronounced
as follows:

s is pronounced like modern English **s** at the beginning of a word, at the end
of a word, or if it is next to an unvoiced consonant within a word (an
unvoiced consonant is one where the vocal cords are not vibrating—try pronouncing **s** and **z** slowly with your finger on your voice-box to feel the difference in vibration between the two).

s is pronounced like modern English **z** if it comes between two vowels or
between a vowel and a voiced consonant (one where the vocal cords
vibrate) within a word.

f is pronounced like modern English **f** at the beginning of a word, at the end
of a word, or if it is next to an unvoiced consonant within a word.

f is pronounced like modern English **v** if it comes between two vowels or
between a vowel and a voiced consonant within a word.

þ and **ð** are pronounced like modern English **th** in the word **thin** (i.e., the
unvoiced sound) at the beginning of a word, at the end of a word, or if next
to an unvoiced consonant within a word.

þ and **ð** are pronounced like modern English **th** in the word **that** (i.e., the
voiced sound) between two vowels or between a vowel and a voiced consonant within a word.

3) The letter **h** is pronounced just like modern English **h** if it occurs at the
beginning of a word.

If it occurs after a vowel, it is pronounced as a kind of rough breathing, with
the tongue tense and pressed towards, but not touching, the roof of the
mouth. The actual sound depends on what kind of a vowel it comes after:

if it is after a vowel that is pronounced at the front of the mouth (for example, **i** or **e**), it is also pronounced at the front of the mouth, and sounds like the consonant you hear in the German word **ich** (if you don't know German, you can approximate this sound by pronouncing the **sh** sound of modern English with your teeth farther apart, your lips laxer, and your tongue quite a bit tenser and closer to your teeth);

if it is after a vowel that is pronounced at the back of the mouth (for example, **o** or **a**), it is also pronounced at the back of the mouth, and sounds like the Scots pronunciation of the last consonant sound in the word **loch**.

4) The letter **c** is pronounced with a **k** sound if it comes before a back vowel (like **o** or **a**) or another consonant. If it comes before a front vowel (like **i** or **e**), or at the end of a word following a front vowel, it is usually pronounced like modern English **ch** in **child**. In this text, any Old English letter **c** that is to be pronounced like modern English **ch** is dotted: **ċ**.

5) The letter **g** is pronounced with a "hard" g sound (i.e., the sound in the modern English words **give** and **grape**) if it comes before a back vowel (like **o** or **a**) or another consonant. If it comes before a front vowel (like **i** or **e**), or at the end of a word following a front vowel, it is usually pronounced like modern English **y** in **yes** or **yellow**. In this text, any Old English letter **g** that is to be pronounced like modern English **y** is dotted: **ġ**.

6) In combinations of consonants, all of the consonants are pronounced, so for example the word **cniht** starts with a **k** sound, followed by an **n** sound.

Some combinations of consonant letters have special values:

The combination **sc** should be pronounced like modern English **sh,** so the Old English words **fisc** and **scip** are pronounced like modern English **fish** and **ship**. An exception to this rule happens when **s** is accidentally followed by **c** in a compound word: **īscald** ("ice-cold") is pronounced with separate **s** and **k** sounds.

The combination **cg** should be pronounced like modern English **dg** in a word like **judge**, so the Old English word **ecg** is pronounced just like the modern English word **edge**.

Pronunciation of Vowel Sounds

1) Short vowels (Again, we'll start with the easy part.)

The following short vowels are pronounced in Old English in much the same way as they are in modern English:

Short **e**, **i** are pronounced like the vowels in **bet** and **bit**.
Short **u** is pronounced like the vowel in **put** or **foot**.
Short **o** is pronounced like the **o** in **pot**.
Short **a** is pronounced like the first **a** of **aha**, or the **a** in **father**.
Short **æ** is pronounced like the vowel in **hat**, **man**, or **cap**, in the North
  American pronunciation of those words.
Short **y** is a high rounded front vowel. This concept is easiest to grasp
  in extended pronunciation, which is explained below for the long
  equivalent. Short **y** is like long **y**, but pronounced for a shorter time.

2) Long vowels

The concept of *long vowel* is often obscured for students because some school-teachers still refer to modern English vowels like the **a** in **game** as "long." These so-called long vowels in modern English are actually not long at all, so please begin by banishing all such preconceptions. Old English long vowels differ from the short vowels primarily because they are actually pronounced for a longer time, not, primarily, because they have a different sound than the corresponding short vowels (even though some of them actually are slightly different in quality when short). In this text, long vowels are indicated with a bar over the letter: **ī**, **ē**, **ā**, etc.

Another problem with learning these pronunciations is the fact that a massive sound change (called the Great Vowel Shift) happened to the English vowel system some time after the Anglo-Saxon period, which creates a huge difference between the way the Anglo-Saxons spelled (and therefore pronounced) vowel sounds and the way we do. Old English vowels are more like continental European vowels than they are like modern English vowels. From this point of view, it is easier to learn Old English if your first language is French or Italian than if your first language is English. Nevertheless, the following series of vowels is not too hard to get hold of if you try:

Long ā is pronounced like the second **a** in **aha**, or like an extended version of the **a** in **father**.

Long ē is pronounced like an extended version of the **a** in **name**, except that if you listen closely to yourself saying the **a** in **name** slowly, you will hear a slight change towards an **ee** sound (as in **teeth**) at the end, which the Old English vowel does not have.

Long ī is pronounced like an extended version of the **i** in **machine**.

Long ō is pronounced like an extended version of the **o** in **boat**, except that if you listen closely to yourself saying that **o** slowly, you will hear a slight change towards an **oo** sound (as in **hoot**) at the end, which the Old English vowel does not have.

Long ū is pronounced like an extended version of the **oo** in **fool**.

Long ȳ is, like its short counterpart, a high rounded front vowel. We don't have one of these in modern English, so if you don't know other languages you may not have encountered it. (It's like the **u** in French **tu**, but extended.) To make it, first notice how your lips are rounded when you say a vowel like the **oo** in **fool**; then notice where your tongue is when you say the **ee** sound in a word like *keep*. Keeping your tongue in that same position and saying **ee**, gradually round your lips to the **oo** position. When your lips are rounded, you have the sound—if you've kept your tongue saying **ee**.

Long ǣ is pronounced like a hard, flat American **a**, as in **flat**, **man**, **hat**, and so on, but for a longer time.

3) Diphthongs

A diphthong is a glide from one vowel sound to another, pronounced as a single syllable. (Be especially careful not to pronounce diphthongs as more than one syllable.)

An example of a diphthong in modern English is the sound roughly like **eeoo** in the word **you**, the word **beautiful**, and the first syllable of **future**—say it very slowly and you'll see that it's made of two vowel sounds, but pronounced as a single syllable.

Students who are not able to access the sound files for the course and do not have a teacher may have difficulty working out an acceptable pronunciation for Old English diphthongs, but the following indications should help:

The diphthong **ea** / **ēa** begins with an **æ** sound and glides to an **a** sound (both as defined above for Old English), with the emphasis on the first sound. In most words, it is no tragedy to pronounce the diphthong simply as an Old English æ, since even Old English scribes could not always distinguish these sounds.

The diphthong **eo** / **ēo** begins with an **e** sound and glides to an **o** sound (both as defined above for Old English), with the emphasis on the first sound.

The diphthong **ie** / **īe** begins with an **i** sound and glides to an **e** sound (both as defined above for Old English), with the emphasis on the first sound.

EXERCISES:

Pronunciation exercises for this chapter are available on the website associated with the text. In addition, you should listen along with the sound files for one of the shorter reading texts, such as the story of Abraham and Isaac, to get a feel for the sounds of the language in running speech.

Chapter 3
Strong Nouns and an Introduction to Old English Cases

[handwritten margin notes: declension – the variation of the form of a noun, pronoun, or adjective]

◆

In contrast to modern English, which with a few exceptions has only one noun declension, Old English had a number of different declensions. Luckily for students, the most common declension is rather similar to our modern English noun declension. Take for example the old English word **cyning** (king). It forms its plural by adding the suffix **-as**, making **cyningas** (kings). And it forms its singular possessive by adding the suffix **-es**, making **cyninges** (king's; of or belonging to a king). The plural possessive is strikingly different from modern English, though. In modern English we write **kings'** (which is pronounced exactly the same as the possessive singular **king's** and the plural **kings**). Instead, Old English adds an **-a** suffix: **cyninga**.

We can express the relationship between these four forms as a table:

Number: Case:	*Singular*	*Plural*
Nominative	**cyning**	**cyningas**
Genitive	**cyninges**	**cyninga**

The words that are new in the table, *nominative* and *genitive*, refer to the form used for the subject of a sentence and the form used for possession, respectively. We use these terms because the Old English nominative and genitive cases have uses other than for sentence subject and possession, uses which will be introduced later in this text.

A table like this, sometimes referred to as a *paradigm*, is the standard way of showing the patterns of noun, pronoun, and adjective declensions. Here, it shows a pattern that is followed by all the Old English nouns (a large number of them) that are of the same class as **cyning**. For example, here is the same table, but with the Old English noun **stān** (stone) instead of **cyning**:

Number:	Singular	Plural
Case:		
Nominative	**stān**	**stānas**
Genitive	**stānes**	**stāna**

And here's the table with **biscop** (bishop—remember the pronunciation of **sc**?) instead of **stān**:

Number:	Singular	Plural
Case:		
Nominative	**biscop**	**biscopas**
Genitive	**biscopes**	**biscopa**

From these tables for **cyning**, **stān**, and **biscop**, you can see two important things. First, the plain form of the word is always the nominative singular form—this will be the form to use to look up words in dictionaries and glossaries. Second, and this is crucial for your success in Old English, once you know what pattern a word follows, you can easily figure out all of its various forms, including the nominative singular (dictionary) form.

Gender in Old English

The pattern we have been exploring with **cyning**, **stān**, and **biscop** is the *strong masculine noun* pattern. *Strong* simply means that compared to some nouns, there are quite a few inflectional changes (here, different endings) in the pattern. It is worth exploring what *masculine* means in some greater detail, however.

Old English nouns had what is known as *grammatical gender*. This concept is sometimes a hard one to grasp at first unless you've already encountered it in a modern language such as French or German, but all it really means is that there are three different sets of noun types in Old English, and that modifiers (e.g., adjectives) and replacing pronouns have different sets of forms for each of the sets of noun types.

The sets of noun types are called *masculine, feminine,* and *neuter*, but there is not any absolute relation between these conventional labels for the word categories and the objects, persons, or animals that the nouns refer to. For example, **þæt wīf**, which means "the woman," is a neuter noun, and **se**

wīfmann, which also means "the woman," is a masculine noun. It is especially common to see nouns that refer to inanimate objects but are grammatically gendered masculine or feminine.

This is only a hard concept to understand if you get too hung up on the idea of "gender." Modern English has "natural gender," such that (by and large) we use **she** to refer to people or animals who really are female, **he** to refer to people or animals who really are male, and **it** to refer to inanimate objects or abstract concepts. Moreover, our nouns do not have grammatical gender, in the sense that all of the articles, adjectives, and so on, that modify them are unaffected by our perception of their genderedness. In Old English the situation is the opposite, almost. The gender of modifiers and of pronouns with noun antecedents is determined largely by the gender of the noun to which they refer, which does not necessarily have any implication about the sex of the object or person being referred to.

Strong Neuter and Feminine Nouns

The most common classes of Old English nouns are the strong masculine nouns like **cyning**, the strong neuter nouns, and the strong feminine nouns. If you learn the endings of these three classes, you will be well on your way to a working knowledge of Old English. Partial paradigms (including only nominative and genitive cases) for strong neuter nouns and for strong feminine nouns are as follows:

Neuter nouns—the model is **bearn** (child):

Number:	*Singular*	*Plural*
Case:		
Nominative	**bearn**	**bearn**
Genitive	**bearnes**	**bearna**

Feminine nouns—the model is **brȳd** (bride):

Number:	*Singular*	*Plural*
Case:		
Nominative	**brȳd**	**brȳda**
Genitive	**brȳde**	**brȳda**

Take a careful look at the paradigms above and notice at least one thing: the alleged importance of case endings in indicating number and sentence role breaks down a bit in these two tables. In the neuter noun paradigm,

[handwritten margin notes: "noun, pronoun, and adj. used for the subj of verb" and "possesive case"]

there is no difference between the nominative singular and the nominative plural; in the feminine paradigm, there is no difference between the nominative plural and the genitive plural. In fact, this is fairly often true in Old English, with the result that two other linguistic features have to take over the function of noun case endings when those are ambiguous: word order (which linguists call syntax) and the forms of other words, including modifiers.

The Masculine *se*-Demonstrative

The most common word accompanying an Old English noun that helps to indicate its case and number is what Old English scholars usually call, somewhat misleadingly, a "demonstrative pronoun." In fact, these words usually do not work like modern English demonstratives (**that, those**) or pronouns (**he, who**), but most often rather like the modern English article (the.) They almost always precede the noun, and they indicate that the noun they modify has been mentioned before or is otherwise specific—which is just what the article **the** does in modern English. Because they do also perform the functions of both demonstratives and demonstrative pronouns, however, this text will refer to them simply as *demonstratives*.

The masculine demonstrative has the following paradigm:

Number:	*Singular*	*Plural*
Case:		
Nominative	**se**	**þā**
Genitive:	**þæs**	**þāra**

Adding demonstratives to the masculine noun paradigm produces the following:

Number:	*Singular*	*Plural*
Case:		
Nominative	**se cyning**	**þā cyningas**
Genitive	**þæs cyninges**	**þāra cyninga**

Notice that the nominative singular demonstrative goes with the nominative singular noun, and so on. This is a fundamental principle of Old English grammar, sometimes called "case harmony": a noun and all its modifiers share the same case and number.

Word Order in Old English

Now that you know the inflections of a few nouns and their demonstratives, you can begin to make and understand simple phrases. One thing you should realize in doing so, and when you come to read Old English texts, is that the case endings and other inflections of Old English do a lot of work that in modern English is done by word order. The result is that word order in Old English is a lot freer and less strictly patterned. Modern English uses word order rather than inflectional change to get across a lot of its meaning:

> The man **on the bench** dropped the cat.
> The man dropped the cat **on the bench**.

> **Bob** reprimanded **Alice**.
> **Alice** reprimanded **Bob**.

Old English word order can be changed dramatically, with a resulting change in meaning that affects emphasis only, rather than basic sense. For example, the Old English sentences below all mean "The king gave his bishop a ring," though the emphasis varies from sentence to sentence:

> Se cyning ġeaf his biscope bēag.
> Bēag ġeaf se cyning his biscope.
> His biscope ġeaf se cyning bēag.
> Se cyning bēag ġeaf his biscope.
> His biscope bēag ġeaf se cyning.

In the combinations you will be building in the exercise below, try using different word orders. For example, the expressions **se bēag þæs cyninges** and **þæs cyninges bēag** mean pretty much the same thing: "the king's ring." But note that even here there are rules: the combination ***þæs cyninges se bēag** needs to be marked with an asterisk to show that it is not good Old English, just as ***the king's the ring** is bad modern English (a noun modified by a possessive phrase does not also take a demonstrative, since "the king's" specifies what ring we are talking about).

EXERCISE 3A:

The following nouns are all strong masculine nouns, so they all follow the same pattern as **cyning**. Build partial paradigms for three or four of them showing singular and plural number and nominative and genitive cases, on the model of the partial paradigms introduced in this chapter. Include the appropriate forms of the demonstrative.

hlāford (lord)   **ramm** (ram,   **eorl** (man, nobleman)
                         i.e., male sheep)

wulf (wolf)   **horn** (horn)   **fēond** (enemy)

stōl (stool)   **bēag** (ring)   **helm** (helmet)

ġebēor (drinking   **smiŏ** (craftsman)   **æþeling** (prince, noble)
buddy)

EXERCISE 3B: *-as → plural   -es → poss sing.   a → poss. plural*

Translate the following Old English phrases involving strong masculine nouns into modern English, using the vocabulary in this chapter and in Exercise 3A and your knowledge of the nominative and genitive cases (refer to the paradigms in the chapter if you need to refresh your memory):

1. þæs cyninges bēag *the king's ring → the ring of the king*
2. þæs biscopes fēond *the bishop's enemy*
3. se stān þæs bēages *the stone the ring's → the ring's stone*
4. þā ġebēoras þæs æþelinges *the drinking buddies the prince's* *gen*
5. þæs rammes hornas *the ram's horns*
6. þāra cyninga fēond *the kings' enemy*
7. se biscop þāra eorla *the bishop the noblemen → the noblemen's body*
8. se stōl þæs smiŏes *→ the stool the craftsman's → the craftsman's stool*
9. þāra wulfa rammas *– the wolves' rams*
10. þæs cyninges bēages stān *the king's ring's stone*

EXERCISE 3C:

Using the vocabulary in Exercise 3A and the chapter, and taking the phrases in Exercise 3B as models, make your own meaningful Old English phrases combining nominatives and genitives, and using demonstratives.

→ underlined → nom plural

dative – indirect obj
accusative – direct obj

Chapter 4
Demonstratives;
Nominative and Genitive Cases

◆

Feminine and Neuter Demonstratives

In the previous chapter we added demonstratives to masculine nouns to form short noun phrases such as **se cyning** and **þā stānas**. Now we will use demonstratives with feminine and neuter nouns and learn a little more about what demonstratives do. We have already noted that demonstratives can act much as the modern English **the** article does, to indicate that we're talking about a specific king, stone, bishop, or wolf, usually one that has been mentioned before. But because demonstratives are inflected for case, number, and gender, another important function they serve is to carry that kind of information. This might seem like duplication of effort, since nouns have gender and are also inflected for case and number. However, sometimes the form of a noun itself does not tell us what its case is, or whether it is singular or plural, and in those cases the demonstrative is really helpful.

In the neuter and feminine paradigms, you can see how adding the demonstrative helps us (and helped Old English speakers) tell the difference between otherwise identical word forms:

Neuter:

Number:	Singular	Plural
Case:		
Nominative	þæt bearn	þā bearn
Genitive	þæs bearnes	þāra bearna

36

Feminine:

Number:	Singular	Plural
Case:		
Nominative	**sēo brȳd**	**þā brȳda**
Genitive	**þǣre brȳde**	**þāra brȳda**

Notice how the addition of demonstratives makes it possible, now, to tell the difference between "the child" (**þæt bearn**) and "the children" (**þā bearn**), and between nominative "the brides" (**þā brȳda**) and genitive "the brides'; of the brides" (**þāra brȳda**), forms that are otherwise identical. Notice also that the forms of the demonstrative for the plural are the same for all three genders, **þā** for nominative and **þāra** for genitive.

Meanings and Uses of the se-Demonstrative

Called after its masculine nominative singular form, the **se**-demonstrative has three main uses. First, a noun phrase with its demonstrative contrasts with the same noun phrase without a demonstrative in much the same way that modern English **the** contrasts with **a**:   se= the

Se æþeling wæs þæs cyninges brōþor.	(The prince was the king's brother.)
Æþeling wæs cyninges brōþor.	(A prince was a king's brother.)
Eorl is ġeþyldig.	(A man is patient.)
Se eorl is ġeþyldig.	(The man is patient.)

Note that the absence of a demonstrative is like using **a** or **an** in front of a modern English word: it creates a general statement or refers to an unknown individual. Although Old English has the words **an** (one, a) and **sum** (a certain, a), both of which sometimes act rather like a modern English indefinite article, they are rather rarely used for this purpose: the demonstrative is simply left off.

The demonstrative can also have a slightly stronger sense, much like modern English **that** or **those**, of picking out individuals for attention:

Se ramm is mara, and se ramm is læssa.	(That ram is bigger, and that ram is smaller.)

Presumably in such use, Old English speakers would emphasize the demonstrative more, just as we stress the word **that** a little bit each time in the corresponding modern English sentence.

Finally, the demonstrative can sometimes be used all by itself, just as we use the modern English demonstrative pronoun **that** or the personal pronouns **he, she, it,** and so on—and with similar meanings:

[Example:]

Þæt wæs gōd cyning.	(That was a good king.)
Se is mīn broþur.	(He—literally, "that one"—is my brother.)

The Nominative Case: Uses

The main use of the nominative case is for the subject of a sentence:

Se æþeling wæs þǣre cwēne fēond.	(The prince was the enemy of the queen.)
Se wulf ofslōg mīne rammas.	(That wolf killed my rams.)
Þæt wīf wæs swīðe wīs.	(The woman was very wise.)

The nominative is also used for direct address (**Lēofa fæder!** "Dear father!"), and it is used when a noun in the predicate is linked to (that is, said to be the same as) the subject by a verb such as "to be" (**bēon** in Old English):

Ælfred is **se cyning** ealra Westseaxna. (Alfred is the king of all West Saxons.)

The Genitive Case: Uses

We have seen that the genitive case is used for possession. It has a wide variety of other uses, but most of them can be easily figured out by translating using either a modern English possessive or a prepositional phrase with **of**:

þæs landes sceawung
(inspection **of the land**—inspection is not possessed by the land, but is an action of the person doing the inspection)

Grendles gryre
(the terror **of Grendel**—Grendel is a monster; his terror is not his possession but something he causes in others)

bēaga weard
(lord **of the rings**—a poetic expression for a ruler, "lord of the rings" because he gives them to his men to reward their service in battle)

There are a few uses of the genitive that just have to be learned, since they are idiomatic. Probably the most common one is the use of the plural genitive with words such as **fela** (much, many) and with large numbers:

fela **fēonda**
(many enemies—literally "many *of* enemies")

þrītig **eorla**
(thirty men—literally "thirty *of* men")

Reading passage

The following short passage has been simplified for your pronunciation practice and your practice in using the nominative and genitive cases. It is based on an entry in the *Anglo-Saxon Chronicle*, a year-by-year history of England that was first compiled during the reign of King Alfred the Great (who died in 899 CE). The entry describes one of his battles, when he had not yet succeeded his brother as king, with invading Danish armies. In this text the word **eorl**, rather than simply meaning "man," refers to a war leader with the rank of nobility called "jarl" in Old Norse, the language of the Vikings.

Text

Se here þāra wīcinga cōm tō Æscesdūne on Westseaxe. Æþelred Cyning and Ælfred þæs cyninges brōþor rīdon up and fuhton wiþ þone here. Se here wæs on twæm ġefylcum. Æþelred fēaht wiþ þāra cyninga here, and Ælfred þæs cyninges brōþor fēaht wiþ þāra eorla here. Se cyning Bagsecg wearþ ofslaġen, and fēower þāra eorla, and þā Deniscan herġas wæron ġefliemde.

Vocabulary

here (strong masculine noun): army, division (a term used of foreign troops)
wīcing (strong masculine noun): Viking
cōm: came
tō: to
Æscesdūn: Ashdown (Berkshire)
Westseaxe: Wessex
Æþelred: Aethelred, Alfred's elder brother
rīdon (plural verb): rode
fuhton (plural verb): fought
on twæm gefylcum: in two divisions
þone (se-demonstrative in accusative case): the
fēaht (singular verb): fought
wearþ ofslaġen: was killed.
fēower: four
herġas: nominative plural of **here**
ġefliemde: put to flight, driven away

EXERCISE 4A:
The following nouns are strong neuter and feminine nouns. Choose at least two of them (one each of neuter and feminine) and construct a partial paradigm showing nominative and genitive cases and both singular and plural forms. Include the appropriate demonstrative form with each noun form.

Neuter:
    land (land)   **wīf** (woman, wife)
    folc (people, nation)   **wæpen** (weapon)
Feminine:
    cwēn (queen)   **sorg** (sorrow, pain)
    tīd (time)   **dūn** (mountain)

EXERCISE 4B:

Using the vocabulary from Exercise 4A, translate the following expressions into Old English, remembering to match demonstratives to the case, gender, and number of the nouns they modify:

1. the mountains of that land
2. the woman's weapons
3. the people of those lands
4. a time of sorrow
5. the queen's sorrows
6. the queens' sorrows
7. a land of mountains
8. the people's weapon
9. the bride's people
10. the queen's child

EXERCISE 4C:

Form further Old English phrases of the type used in Exercise 4B, but add some of the masculine nouns you learned in Chapter 3 and its exercises. Try making some phrases with three nouns, e.g., "the mountain of the land of kings," "the weapons of the queen of that land."

Chapter 5
A Few Old English Verbs;
Accusative and Dative Cases

◆

Unlike modern English verbs, almost all of which only have one distinctive form (for the third person present: he **sees** compared to I **see**, you **see**, they **see**, and so on), Old English verbs have distinctive forms for the plural and for the three persons of the singular. It is easiest to learn these forms along with the pronouns that are often their subjects, so this chapter introduces both the Old English personal pronouns and a few Old English verbs.

We will present the conjugation of a verb as a table similar to the noun tables we have seen in previous chapters, showing the different forms and their number and person. Here's the table for the present of the verb **bēon** ("to be"):

	singular	*plural*
1st person	**iċ eom**	**wē sindon**
	(I am)	(we are)
2nd person	**þū eart**	**ġē sindon**
	(you are—singular)	(you are—plural)
3rd person	**hē (hēo, hit) is**	**hīe sindon**
	(he [she, it] is)	(they are)

If you compare the Old English forms to their modern English translations, there are several things to notice. First, some of the forms are very similar to modern English—**wē** is like "we," **hē** is like "he," **is** matches "is," **iċ eom** is a bit similar to "I am"—and others are a bit like forms in old-fashioned English—**þū eart** and "thou art," **ġē** and "ye." So you already know parts of this table. Second, all the plural verb forms are the same, which helps a lot with remembering things. Finally, unlike modern English, which has one pronoun, **you**, that covers both singular and plural, Old English has two, **þū** for speaking to a single person and **ġē** for speaking to more than one person. (In fact, there's a third pronoun form called the *dual* for speaking to a group of two people, for example a married couple, which we'll introduce later.)

To learn the forms of a verb—and the verb **bēon** is one you need to know early because it comes up very frequently—one of the best ways is to memorize the verb forms with the associated pronoun forms. You can make your own flash cards to do this, or you can teach yourself the forms as an oral chant, or you can make a blank verb paradigm on paper or computer, marked with the persons and numbers but without the verb forms filled in, and then attempt to fill in the correct forms from memory until you are able to do so. Which method works for you will depend on what kind of a learner you are. Do remember, though, that even though you are learning the verbs together with pronouns, the third person verbs are very frequently used in actual Old English with nouns rather than pronouns:

	singular	*plural*
3rd person	**se cyning is**	**þā cyningas sindon**

(From this point on in this textbook, the personal pronouns are not added to the verb tables to save space, but please add them yourself when you work at learning the verb forms, because it really helps to remember which form is which if you associate them with the pronouns.)

The Verbs bēon and habban

As in modern English, the verbs **to be** and **to have** are very common indeed, and your progress in learning Old English will suffer if you don't learn them right away. Here are the paradigms for the present and *preterite* (past tense) forms:

bēon (to be)

present	*singular*	*plural*
1st person	**eom, bēo**	**sind(on), bēoþ**
2nd person	**eart, bist**	**sind(on), bēoþ**
3rd person	**is, biþ**	**sind(on), bēoþ**

preterite

1st person	**wæs**	**wǣron**
2nd person	**wǣre**	**wǣron**
3rd person	**wæs**	**wǣron**

Where two or more forms are given for one place in the table above, that means that these various forms (for example **eom** and **bēo** for the first person singular) will be found in our texts. Sometimes the reason for finding one form rather than another is clear (as in the case of **sind** instead of **sindon**, where the dialect of the writer is the reason), and sometimes it is less than clear (as in the case of **biþ** rather than **is**, where various theories involving differing meanings or shades of meaning have been proposed).

habban (to have)

present	*singular*	*plural*
1st person	**hæbbe**	**habbaþ**
2nd person	**hæfst, hafast**	**habbaþ**
3rd person	**hæfþ, hafaþ**	**habbaþ**

preterite		
1st person	**hæfde**	**hæfdon**
2nd person	**hæfdest**	**hæfdon**
3rd person	**hæfde**	**hæfdon**

Luckily, the similarities to modern English and (in the case of **habban**, especially) the simplicity of the paradigms make them easy to remember. Also as in modern English, these verbs are used both as main sentence verbs (**Þæt wæs gōd cyning**—that was a good king) and as auxiliary verbs in connection with the Old English equivalents of our present participle (the -ing form) and past participle (usually the -ed form):

Hīe wæron feohtende.   (They were fighting OR They kept fighting.)
Hē hæfde hafoc onfongne.   (He had received a hawk.)

Other Old English Verb Conjugations

There are two main types of verb in Old English, called strong verbs and weak verbs, which follow different conjugations. As mentioned in Chapter 1, strong verbs signal changes in meaning such as from present to past (preterite) by changing their main vowels. Here is an example of a strong verb in present and preterite:

ġiefan (to give)

present	*singular*	*plural*
1st person	ġiefe	ġiefaþ
2nd person	ġiefst	ġiefaþ
3rd person	ġiefþ	ġiefaþ

preterite		
1st person	ġeaf	ġēafon
2nd person	ġēafe	ġēafon
3rd person	ġeaf	ġēafon

And here, for contrast, is an example of a weak verb, a class of verbs that is the ancestor of the modern English "regular" verb:

lufian (to love)

present	*singular*	*plural*
1st person	lufie	lufiaþ
2nd person	lufast	lufiaþ
3rd person	lufaþ	lufiaþ

preterite		
1st person	lufode	lufodon
2nd person	lufodest	lufodon
3rd person	lufode	lufodon

Compare the two paradigms, and notice that where ġiefan changes its stem vowel from ie to ea (or ēa) to form the preterite, lufian adds a different series of suffixes, for example -odest instead of -ast. Verbs that are constructed using suffixes, like lufian, are called weak verbs, while verbs that change their vowels, like ġiefan, are called strong verbs. In modern English, the descendants of some of the Old English strong verbs are called "irregular verbs," but there are far too many strong verbs in Old English and too many regularities among them for the term "irregular" to be accurate.

Transitive Verbs and Their Objects: Accusative and Dative Cases

Verbs that have grammatical objects are called *transitive verbs*. In most cases, a transitive verb will have only one object. In Old English, that object is usually in the *accusative case*:

Hēo lufode þone cyning.	(She loved the king.)
Se biscop hæfde cniht.	(The bishop had a servant.)
Hæfst þū hafoc?	(Do you have a hawk?)

(Some verbs "take" the genitive or dative case for their object, but these are special cases to be discussed later.)

When there are two objects, a *direct object* and an *indirect object*, the direct object is in the accusative case, the indirect object in the *dative case* (these can occur in any order):

Se cyning him ġeaf bēagas.	(The king gave him rings.)
Se hunta ġeaf his bearne bārspere.	(The hunter gave his child a boar-spear.)

Accusative and Dative Cases: Strong Masculine Nouns

Here is the full paradigm for strong masculine nouns, with the dative and accusative cases added and demonstratives supplied:

Strong Masculine Noun
cyning (king)

	Singular	*Plural*
Nominative	se cyning	þā cyningas
Accusative	þone cyning	þā cyningas
Genitive	þæs cyninges	þāra cyninga
Dative	þǣm cyninge	þǣm cyningum

Reading passage

This passage is adapted from the voyage of the merchant Ohthere to the country of the Biarmians in Northern Europe, as recounted in the Old English translation of a history of the world by Orosius. The story of the voyage is awkardly inserted into the early part of the translation, presumably to extend Orosius's summary of world geography with information that had recently been learned at the court of King Alfred. The entire text of the voyage of Ohthere is one of the readings at the back of this book.

Text

Ohthere ġeaf his hlaforde, Ælfrede Cyninge, sume tēþ hwæla. Hē wæs swīþe spēdiġ mann. Hē hæfde hrānas. Hē hæfde syx hund tamra hrāna unbebohtra. Þā tēþ wǣron tēþ þāra hwæla þe horshwælas sindon ġenemnode. Þā horshwælas habbað swīðe æþele bān in hira tōþum. Hē sæde þæt hē sohte Beormas in Beorma lande. Hē sæde þæt hē fōr þider for þǣm horshwælum. Þā Beormas him sædon fela spella.

Vocabulary

Ohthere (proper name): Ohthere
hlaforde (masc noun, dat sing): lord
Ælfrede (masc proper name, dat sing): Alfred
sume: some
hwæla (masc noun, gen sing): of whales, whales'
tēþ: teeth
swīþe: very
spēdiġ: wealthy
mann: man
hrān (masc noun): reindeer

syx hund: six hundred
tamra ... unbebohtra: tame ... unsold
horshwæl (masc noun): walrus (literally, "horse whale")
ġenemnode: called, named
æþele: noble, excellent
bān: bone, ivory
hira: their
tōþum: teeth (dat pl)
sæde (sing), **sædon** (pl): said
þæt: that (conj)
sohte: visited
Beormas (masc proper noun): the Biarmians, a northern European culture
    about which little is known
lande (neut noun, dat sing): land, country
fōr: travelled
þider: there, to that place, thither
fela: many
spella (neut noun, gen pl): of stories

EXERCISE 5A:
Write out a complete verb paradigm for **bēon** and one for **habban** by adding
the appropriate personal pronoun subjects to both the present and the preterite
tenses of each verb.

EXERCISE 5B:
The accusative forms of the personal pronouns are as follows:

	singular	*plural*
first person	**mē** (me)	**ūs** (us)
second person	**þē** (you, sing)	**ēow** (you, pl)
third person	**hine** (him), **hīe** (her), **hit** (it)	**hīe** (them)

Make five different sentences using nominative and accusative pronouns and
the verb **lufian**, for example "Iċ lufie þē" (I love you). Make sure you use both
present and preterite tenses and both plural and singular verbs and pronouns
in the course of your five sentences. Remember that the form of the verb
depends on the person and number of its subject, not its object, and that the
object needs to be in the accusative case, the subject in the nominative.

EXERCISE 5C:
Translate the following sentences into modern English. They use the familiar nouns **cyning**, **biscop**, **bēag**, **hafoc**, and **stān**, all strong masculines, and the verb **ġiefan**.

1. Se cyning ġeaf þǣm biscope bēag.
2. Þā biscopas ġēafon þǣm cyninge hafoc.
3. Þæs cyninges hafoc ġiefþ bēag þǣm biscopum.
4. Þǣm biscope ġeaf se cyning bēag.
5. Hafocas ġiefaþ þā stānas biscope.
6. Wē ġeafon hafocas biscopum þæs cyninges.
7. Hē ġeaf hit þǣm cyninge.
8. Biscopum ġeaf se cyning bēagas.
9. Þǣm biscope ġiefaþ hafocas þone bēag.
10. Ġiefaþ ġē stānas þǣm cyninge?

Chapter 6
Weak Verbs:
Subjunctive, Participles, Infinitives

◆

The verb **lufian**, introduced in the previous chapter, is a representative weak verb, one of a very large class of verbs in Old English that are all conjugated the same way (with only a few variations). These verbs form their past (preterite) tense by substitution of a suffix containing a **d**; they are the ancestors of the regular verbs of modern English, which form their past tense by adding **-ed** to the present form. This chapter introduces the full conjugation of **lufian** and explains some of the "parts" of weak verbs such as participles, infinitives, and the subjunctive, which we have not yet encountered.

Conjugation of lufian

lufian (to love)

	singular	plural
indicative		
present	*singular*	*plural*
1st person	**lufie**	**lufiaþ**
2nd person	**lufast**	**lufiaþ**
3rd person	**lufaþ**	**lufiaþ**
preterite		
1st person	**lufode**	**lufodon**
2nd person	**lufodest**	**lufodon**
3rd person	**lufode**	**lufodon**

subjunctive

present	*singular*	*plural*
1st person	**lufie**	**lufien**
2nd person	**lufie**	**lufien**
3rd person	**lufie**	**lufien**

preterite		
1st person	**lufode**	**lufoden**
2nd person	**lufode**	**lufoden**
3rd person	**lufode**	**lufoden**

imperative		
	lufa	**lufiaþ**

infinitive
lufian, tō lufienne

present participle
lufiende

past participle
(ġe)lufod

Some variations you should know about:

1. The **o** in the **-ode** ending (etc.) of the preterite may well appear as **e** or **a**.
2. A certain number of weak verbs do not have the **i** of the **-ian** infinitive ending there or throughout the present (indicative and subjunctive). Standard examples are the verb **fremman** (to make, do), whose present tense has **fremme, fremest, fremeþ**, and **fremmaþ**, and **hīeran** (to hear, obey), which has **hīere, hīerst, hīerþ, hīeraþ**.

Imperative and Subjunctive

Old English has three verb *moods*: the *indicative, subjunctive,* and *imperative.* We do have these in modern English as well, although the subjunctive has almost disappeared except for very rare idiomatic situations (for example, "I wish I were dead," where most people now substitute the past tense, "I wish I was dead").

The imperative mood is used only for direct commands:

Ġecnāwaþ þæt sōð is!   (**Recognize** what is true!)

The indicative mood is the one most often used by far, and the one we have been using exclusively to this point. By and large, it is used for situations when facts and reality, as opposed to guesses, wishes, or imagined situations, are the content of a sentence or clause.

The subjunctive mood will be more fully explored in a subsequent chapter, but it generally signals that the action or state specified by the verb is the object of a wish, a hope, or a fear, a command or request, a conjecture, belief or hypothesis, or is for some other reason unreal. The subjunctive cannot usually be the mood of the verb of a main clause (except in the case of sentences expressing a wish amounting to a command):

Wish:
Iċ wolde ðætte hīe ealneġ æt ðǣre stōwe **wǣren**.
   (I prefer that they always **be** at that place.)
Belief:
Iċ ġelīefe ðæt ðū **wille**.
   (I believe that you **want to**.)
Conjecture:
Iċ wēne þætte noht moniġe beġiondan Humbre **nǣren**.
   (I guess that there **may not have been** many beyond the Humber.)

In the absence of a full explanation of the subjunctive (for which see Chapter 11), you might think of that part of the verb conjugation paradigm as if each verb form were preceded by a statement of belief: "Iċ ġelīefe þæt iċ lufie" ("I believe that I love"), "Iċ ġelīefe þæt þū lufie" ("I believe that you love"), and so on.

Infinitives

The infinitive of a verb is its "dictionary form"; that is, verbs are listed using this form in dictionaries and glossaries. In modern English, the infinitive is the form used with **to**: **to love**, **to give**, and so on. We can often create a good translation of Old English by using the modern English equivalent with **to**:

God wolde **fandian** Abrahames gehiersumnesse.
(God wanted **to test** Abraham's obedience.)
Abraham hēt Isaac **beran** þone wudu.
(Abraham commanded Isaac **to bear** [i.e., carry] the wood.)

As in these examples, we most often find infinitives in our texts in combination with other verbs, such as Old English auxiliary verbs **sculan** (ought to), **motan** (may), **willan** (want to), and other verbs such as **hātan** (to command) and **sēon** (to see). One difference between Old English infinitives and their modern English counterparts is that the Old English infinitive, especially with verbs involving commands and perception, can have a passive rather than an active sense:

Iċ ġesawe trēow on lyft **lǣdan**.
(I saw a tree **to be carried**—we would translate "saw a tree carried"—into the air.)

[Hē] hēt up **beran** æþelinga gestrēon.
(He commanded the treasure of princes **to be carried** up.)

Besides the plain form of the infinitive, Old English has an *inflected infinitive*, formed with **tō**, such as **tō lufienne** in the paradigm in this chapter. There is no real distinction in meaning between the plain and inflected infinitive, but the inflected form is used with **bēon, habban**, adjectives, and nouns, and not usually with the auxiliaries mentioned above.

Sorh is mēā **to secganne**.
(Sorrow is to me—i.e., "it is a sorrow to me"—**to say**.)

Participles

The present and past participles in modern English are the **-ing** and **-ed** forms (in regular verbs—irregular verbs may have forms without **-ed** for the past participle, such as *chosen*). Their most common use is in forming compound verb tenses: **was loving, had loved, will have loved, had been loving**. They are also used as adjectives, either in the predicate or modifying a noun:

The **relaxing** music **was sounding** increasingly **irritating** to her.
Completed forms **were deposited** in the box **marked** "forms."

Both of these uses, as adjective and as part of a compound verb, are also in
Old English, although Old English much more frequently uses a simple
present or preterite tense where we might use a compound tense, so in general
adjectival uses of the participles predominate.

Hīe alle **wǣron feohtende** oþþæt hīe **hæfdon** þone cyning **ofslægenne**.
(They all **were fighting** until they **had slain** the king.)

Þū eart mīn **ġelufoda** sunu; in þē iċ ġelīcode.
(You are my beloved son; in you I have been pleased.—The **-a** ending
of **ġelufoda** shows that the past participle **ġelufod** is acting as an
adjective and modifying the masculine nominative singular noun
sunu.)

Þis **lufiende** wīf.
(This **loving** woman.)

Reading Passage

This passage is adapted from the Old English gospel account of the birth of
Jesus (Luke 2). A more complete text appears as a reading passage at the back
of this book. Some readers will be surprised to learn that the Bible was translated from Latin into English so early, because a common myth is that translation of the Bible into English only took place with the rise of Protestantism.
In fact, important parts of the Bible had been translated into English some 600
years before the King James Version and some 400 years before Wycliffe, a
fact that aroused the first wave of strong scholarly interest in Old English, by
Protestants during the Renaissance. The glossary to this reading selection is
presented in alphabetical order. Note that þ and ð follow t, that æ is listed as
if it were **ae**, and that the prefix **ġe-** is ignored and the word listed under the
following letter.

Text

Sōþliċe on þām dagum wæs ġeworden ġebod fram þām Cāsere Augusto þæt eall ymbehwyrft wǣre tōmearcod. Ða fērde Iosep fram Galilea of þǣre ċeastre Nazareth on ċeastre Dauides sēo is ġenemned Bethleem forþam þe hē wæs of Dauides hūse. He fērde mid Marian þe him beweddod wæs and wæs ġeeacnod. Sōðlice wæs geworden, þā hī þǣr wǣron, hire dagas wǣron ġefyllede þæt hēo cende, and hēo cende hyre frumcennedan sunu and hine mid ċildclāþum bewand and hine on binne ālēde, forþām þe hīġ næfdon rūm on cumena hūse. And hyrdas wǣron on þām ylcan rīċe waciende and nihtwæċċan healdende ofer heora heorda.

Vocabulary

ālecgan: to lay (**ālēde** 3rd pers sing pret indic)
Augustus: Augustus (**Augusto** dat sing)
beweddod (past part): married, betrothed
bewindan (str verb): wind, wrap (**bewand** 3rd pers sing pret indic)
binn (fem noun): bin, manger (**binne** acc sing)
ġebod: decree
Cāsere: Caesar, emperor (**Cāsere** dat sing)
ċeaster: city (**ċeastre** dat sing)
cennan (wk verb): give birth (**cende** 3rd pers sing pret indic)
ċildclāþ (masc noun): baby cloth, swaddling-cloth (**ċildclāþum** dat pl)
cuma (masc noun): guest, stranger (**cumena** gen pl)
dæġ (masc noun): day (**dagas** nom pl, **dagum** dat pl)
Dauid: David (**Dauides** gen sing)
ġeeacnod (past part): increased, made larger; pregnant
eall: all
fēran: go, travel (**fērde** 3rd pers sing pret indic)
forþām þe (conj): because
fram: from, by
frumcennedan (past part acc sing masc): firstborn
ġefyllede (past part nom pl masc): fulfilled
Galilea: Galilee
healdan: to hold, keep (**healdende** pres part)
heora (pers pron gen pl): their
heord (fem noun): herd, flock (**heorda** acc pl)
hī, hīġ (pers pron pl): they

him (pers pron, dat sing): to him
hire (pers pron, gen sing): her
hūs: house (**hūse** dat sing)
hyrde (masc noun): shepherd (**hyrdas** nom pl)
hyre (pers pron, gen sing): her
Iosep: Joseph
Maria: Mary (**Marian** dat sing)
mid (prep): with, along with
næfdon: did not have
ġenemned (past part): named
nihtwæċċe (fem noun): night-watch (**nihtwæċċan** acc sing)
of: from
ofer: over
on: in, into
rīce: kingdom
rūm (masc noun): room
sōþliċe: truly
sunu (masc noun): son
tōmearcod (past part): listed in a census
þā: then, when
þǣr (adv): there
þæt (conj): that
þe (rel pron): who, that
wacian (wk verb): wake, remain awake (**waciende** pres part)
ġeworden (past part of **weorðan**): taken place (**wæs ġeworden**: took place, had taken place)
ylca (adj): same (**ylcan** dat sing neut)
ymbehwyrft: the (circle of the) world, the world considered as a flat disk

EXERCISE 6A:
The weak verb **wacian** in the reading passage is conjugated exactly like **lufian**. Create a table for **wacian** like the one for **lufian** in this chapter, but with pronoun subjects added where a subject is required (remember that infinitives and participles do not take subjects and that imperative forms do not need them).

EXERCISE 6B:
For each of the following weak verb forms conjugated like **lufian**, figure out the person, number, and tense (all are indicative) and provide a translation. In

some cases, there may be more than one possibility for person, and you should state all the possibilities. The verbs used are **ascian** (ask), **andswarian** (answer), **endian** (end), **baþian** (bathe), **fandian** (test), and **smiþian** (make, construct).

1. smiþiaþ
2. ascode
3. andswarodon
4. baþaþ
5. endast
6. andswarodest
7. smiþie
8. endodon
9. ascie
10. fandaþ

EXERCISE 6C:

Using the strong masculine noun paradigm introduced at the end of Chapter 5, construct five sentences using **lufian, ascian, andswarian, baþian,** and **fandian** in which the subject is in the nominative case and the object in the accusative case. Use the nouns **cyning, biscop, stān, bēag,** and so on introduced in Exercise 3A, along with the appropriate demonstratives.

Chapter 7
Strong Nouns and Cases

◆

In previous chapters we briefly explored the strong nouns. In this chapter we will examine the full paradigms of masculine, neuter, and feminine strong nouns and discuss some uses of the Old English cases in more detail.

Noun Paradigms: Strong Masculine, Neuter, and Feminine Nouns

Strong Masculine Noun
cyning (king)

	Singular	*Plural*
Nominative	se cyning	þā cyningas
Accusative	þone cyning	þā cyningas
Genitive	þæs cyninges	þāra cyninga
Dative	þǣm cyninge	þǣm cyningum

Some variations you should know about:

a) many strong masculine nouns end in **-e** in the nominative and accusative singular; this ending is dropped before adding the other case endings.

b) nouns with **æ** as their vowel usually change this to **a** in the plural, so **dæġ** (day) but **dagas** (days).

c) many nouns with two syllables drop the vowel of the second syllable everywhere but in the nominative and accusative singular: **fugol** (bird, nominative singular) but **fugles** (genitive singular), **engel** (angel, accusative singular) but **engla** (genitive plural).

d) the **-um** ending of the dative plural can show up as **-an** or **-on** in later texts.

Strong Neuter Noun
bearn (child)

	Singular	*Plural*
Nominative	þæt bearn	þā bearn
Accusative	þæt bearn	þā bearn
Genitive	þæs bearnes	þāra bearna
Dative	þǣm bearne	þǣm bearnum

Some variations you should know about:
a) many strong neuter nouns have a nominative and accusative plural ending
-u, so that, for example, the nominative plural of **scip** (ship) is **scipu**. (Apparently no longer pronounced distinctly in late Old English, this **-u** ending can also appear as **-o** or even **-a**.)
  The full declension of **scip** looks like this:

	Singular	*Plural*
Nominative	scip	scipu
Accusative	scip	scipu
Genitive	scipes	scipa
Dative	scipe	scipum

b) nouns with **æ** as their vowel usually change this to **a** in the plural: **fæt** (vessel) but **fatu** (vessels).
c) many nouns with two syllables drop the second syllable everywhere but in the nominative and accusative singular, so **hēafod** (head, nominative singular) but **hēafdes** (genitive singular).
d) the **-um** ending of the dative plural can show up as **-an** or **-on** in later texts.

Strong Feminine Noun
brȳd (bride)

	Singular	*Plural*
Nominative	sēo brȳd	þā brȳda
Accusative	þā brȳde	þā brȳda
Genitive	þǣre brȳde	þāra brȳda
Dative	þǣre brȳde	þǣm brȳdum

Some variations you should know about:
a) many strong feminine nouns have the ending **-u** in the nominative singular, for example **ġiefu** (gift), an ending which is dropped before adding the

endings for other cases and numbers. (Apparently no longer pronounced distinctly in late Old English, this ending can also appear as **-o** or even **-a**.)

The full declension of **ġiefu** looks like this:

	Singular	Plural
Nominative	ġiefu	ġiefa
Accusative	ġiefe	ġiefa
Genitive	ġiefe	ġiefa
Dative	ġiefe	ġiefum

b) the ending **-a** for nominative and accusative plural can also appear as **-e** (or even other vowels), and the **-e** ending of the non-nominative cases of the singular sometimes appears as **-a**.

c) words of two syllables sometimes lose the vowel of the second syllable everywhere except in the nominative singular: **ċeaster** (city/castle, nominative singular) but **ċeastre** (accusative singular).

d) the **-um** ending of the dative plural can show up in later texts as **-an** or **-on**.

e) occasionally the ending **-ena** is used for genitive plural rather than **-a**.

Prepositions and Cases

When a noun is the object of a preposition, it will not be in the nominative case but in some other case. What case depends on the preposition: some prepositions "take" (i.e., are normally used with) the dative case, some the accusative case, and a certain number take either the accusative or dative case depending on the meaning. A very few are used with the genitive case. The dative case is the most frequent case for the object of a preposition:

to þām lande	(to the land)
uppan ānre dūne	(upon a mountain)
mid twām cnapum	(with two servants)
ofer his swēoran	(over his neck)

Some prepositions never or almost never appear with any case but the dative: examples are **fram/from** (from, out of) and **mid** (with, by means of). A smaller class of prepositions routinely appear with the accusative case, including **wið** (against) and **þurh** (through). But a lot of prepositions can take either accusative or dative cases depending on the meaning. Normally, the accusative implies motion toward something, whereas the dative refers to a static state:

in þā ċeastre	(accusative— into the city)	in þǣre ċeastre	(dative—in the city)
uppan þā dūne	(accusative— onto the mountain)	uppan þǣre dūne	(dative—upon the mountain)

The most commonly encountered prepositions that operate this way are **in** ("into" with accusative, "in" with dative) and **on** ("onto" with accusative, "on" with dative).

A final, slightly surprising fact about Old English prepositions is that (despite the fact that *preposition* means "something put in front of" something else) they can appear after their objects, particularly in the case of pronouns:

> Hē cwæþ **him tō** ...   (He said **to him** ...)

Be particularly watchful for postposed prepositions (prepositions coming after their objects) in poetry.

Verbs and Cases

The direct object of a verb is most frequently in the accusative case, the indirect object in the dative case, as we saw in Chapter 5. However, a small number of verbs have what we can only understand as direct objects, but in cases other than the accusative. For example, the verb **brūcan** ("to enjoy, use, profit from") is normally associated with the genitive of what is enjoyed:

> Ne mæġ nān **flǣscmetta brūcan** būtan mīnum cræfte.
> (None may **enjoy meat** [literally, "of meats"] without my work.— a salt-maker is speaking)
> Þǣr iċ mōt **drēames brūcan**.
> (There I will be able **to enjoy happiness**.)

Other verbs appear with dative direct objects:

>Se cyning wolde **þām ġelēafan onfōn** þe se biscop lǣrde.
>(The king wanted **to receive** [onfōn] **the faith** [þām ġelēafan] that the bishop taught.)
>Hēo þurh mæġðhād mycclum **ġelīcode þām heofonlīcan cyninge**.
>(She through virginity greatly **pleased the heavenly King**.)

Verbs involving deprivation take the dative of what someone is being deprived of:

>Oft iċ earmċeariġ, **eðle bidǣled**, sohte sinces bryttan.
>(Often I miserable, **deprived of homeland**, sought a treasure-giver.)

Adverbial Uses of Cases

The Instrumental Use of the Dative Case

Old English once had a separate *instrumental case*, but it had almost entirely disappeared by the time our surviving texts were written down. There are two main remainders of it: the demonstrative **þȳ** (also appears as **þe** and **þon**), which occasionally shows up on its own or with the dative singular form of masculine and neuter nouns, and an **-e** adjective ending, again for masculine and neuter singular. In general, the function of the instrumental is served by the dative case, which is acting in an instrumental way when it is used to designate something *by means of which* an action is accomplished:

>Hygewlonc brȳd grapode **hondum**.
>(The proud bride grasped [it] **with** [her] **hands**.)
>Þēodnes dōhtor **hræġle** þeahte þrindende þing.
>(The lord's daughter **with a sheet** covered the swelling thing.)

Such instrumental uses of the dative are very common indeed.

Accusative and Genitive Time Expressions

Both the accusative and the genitive may be used for time expressions. Such a use of the accusative is a special case of its use to designate extents of space, time, and degree (e.g., Him wæs **ealne wēg** wēste land on þæt stēorbord—For him there was **all the way** deserted land on the starboard). The accusative with time expressions refers to **how long** something occurs for:

> **Ealle ðā hwīle** hē sceal siġlian be lande.
> (**All that time** he shall sail by land.)

The genitive case is also used for time expressions. In contrast to the accusative, it forms expressions that refer to the time *during which* something occurs:

> **dæġes** ond **nihtes**
> (during the day and during the night)
> **þæs ġeares** wurdon eahta folcġefeoht ġefohten
> ([during] **that year** eight folk-battles were fought)

EXERCISE 7A:
For each of the following nouns, identify case, number, and gender and state the headword you would look under in a dictionary or glossary to find the word (i.e., the nominative singular form). If there are multiple possible answers (for example, a neuter noun form that could be either nominative or accusative, a genitive plural where you cannot be sure of the gender or therefore of the ending you might find in the dictionary), state all the possibilities. (For your own satisfaction, try looking up any words you do not know here in an Old English dictionary, such as the Clark Hall and Meritt *Concise Anglo-Saxon Dictionary*. Were you right?)

1. scipu
2. ġiefu
3. se þwang
4. þone mete
5. þǣre lāre
6. þā hilde
7. þā land

8. þǣm sciprāpum
9. þāra folca
10. þæt tācen

EXERCISE 7B:

The preposition **þurh** (through) usually takes the accusative for its object, **mid** (with) takes the dative, **in** and **on** can take either dative (location) or accusative (motion towards). For each of the nouns used as paradigms in this chapter (**cyning, bearn, scip, brȳd, ġiefu**) make six prepositional phrases, one each with **þurh** and **mid**, two different ones for both **in** and **on**, all with the appropriate demonstrative.

EXERCISE 7C:

Make five Old English sentences using the verbs **ġiefan**, **lufian**, and **habban**, each of which must include at least one object, one possessive in the genitive, and one prepositional phrase. For example (before translation into Old English): The king of that land gave the bride a ring on the ship.

Chapter 8
Strong Verbs; Personal Pronouns

◆

A large number of the most frequently encountered Old English verbs are strong verbs, those that form their past tense and past participle by changes of vowel and do not add a suffix containing **d** (sometimes **t**) as do the weak verbs. For the beginning student of Old English, especially one who does not plan to become a specialist, it may not make sense to acquire the life-skill of conjugating all seven classes of Old English strong verbs (and there are sub-classes!), but you will still find it useful to get a basic understanding of how they work, if only because it will speed up your reading of the Old English texts. This chapter presents the basic conjugation of strong verbs and looks in particular at some commonly encountered verbs and their sound changes.

Conjugation of a Strong Verb

(Class 3) strong verb **helpan** (to help)

indicative		
present	*singular*	*plural*
1st person	**helpe**	**helpað**
2nd person	**hilpst**	**helpað**
3rd person	**hilpð**	**helpað**

preterite		
1st person	**healp**	**hulpon**
2nd person	**hulpe**	**hulpon**
3rd person	**healp**	**hulpon**

subjunctive
present

1st person	**helpe**	**helpen**
2nd person	**helpe**	**helpen**
3rd person	**helpe**	**helpen**

preterite

1st person	**hulpe**	**hulpen**
2nd person	**hulpe**	**hulpen**
3rd person	**hulpe**	**hulpen**

imperative

help	**helpaþ**

infinitive
helpan, tō helpenne

present participle
helpende

past participle
(ġe)holpen

Sound Changes in the Strong Verb Paradigm

The paradigm above shows how sound changes are distributed. The vowel of the infinitive (here, **helpan**, so **e**) is used in the present indicative (except for second and third persons singular) and present subjunctive, and in the imperative and present participle. A second vowel, **i**, is used in the second and third persons singular of the present indicative. In the preterite (past) tense, two further vowels occur, **ea** in the first and third persons singular, and **u** in the second person singular and the plural of the indicative (as well as throughout the subjunctive). Finally, the past participle, **(ġe)holpen**, has its own vowel.

There are a total of five different vowels here, which are used to help distinguish the different parts of the verb. For example, the difference between "I help" and "I helped" is more strikingly made with the different vowel than with the presence or absence of an **-e** ending: **iċ helpe, iċ healp**. If these five vowel sounds had to be memorized with each verb, Old English would be an extraordinarily difficult language to learn, but in fact, just as modern English has **ring, rang, rung**, and (with the same vowels) **sing, sang, sung**, and **drink, drank**,

drunk (which means that once we get the pattern we have no difficulty with applying it to further verbs), Old English strong verbs come in categories that share vowel progressions. There are seven such classes, commonly called Class 1 to Class 7. Here is a representative verb from each of the classes:

	infinitive	3rd sg pres indic	3rd sg pret indic	pret pl	past part
Class 1:	**rīdan** (to ride)	**rītt**	**rād**	**ridon**	**(ġe)riden**
Class 2:	**drēogan** (to endure, undergo)	**drīehð**	**drēag**	**drugon**	**(ġe)drogen**
Class 3:	**hweorfan** (to turn, go)	**hwierfð**	**hwearf**	**hwurfon**	**(ġe)hworfen**
Class 4:	**beran** (to bear)	**birð**	**bær**	**bǣron**	**(ġe)boren**
Class 5:	**sprecan** (to say, speak)	**spricð**	**spræc**	**sprǣcon**	**(ġe)sprecen**
Class 6:	**faran** (to go)	**færð**	**fōr**	**fōron**	**(ġe)faren**
Class 7:	**healdan** (to hold, own, rule)	**hielt**	**hēold**	**hēoldon**	**(ġe)healden**

It is not quite accurate to consider the examples above as paradigms, because in each case there are other verbs that are considered by grammarians to be in the same class that nevertheless behave somewhat differently. Class 3 is particularly riddled with sub-classes. However, examining the vowel changes above will give you a good idea of the kinds of patterns there are in Old Engish strong verbs. In fact, in this text and its accompanying reader, as in most introductory Old English texts, some dictionaries, and many scholarly editions, the verb forms with altered vowels are cross-referenced to the main glossary entry (which is under the infinitive as headword).

Personal Pronouns: Full Declension

In Chapter 5 we examined the personal pronouns as subjects of verbs, but of course pronouns need to show the various cases of Old English so that they can be (among other things) objects of verbs and prepositions and can indicate possession. The full declension is as follows:

singular

	1st person	*2nd person*
Nominative	iċ	þū
Accusative	mē, meċ	þē, þeċ
Genitive	mīn	þīn
Dative	mē	þē

3rd person	*masculine*	*feminine*	*neuter*
Nominative	hē	hēo, hīo	hit
Accusative	hine	hīe, hī	hit
Genitive	his	hire	his
Dative	him	hire	him

dual

	1st person	*2nd person*
Nominative	wit	ġit
Accusative	unc	inc
Genitive	unċer	inċer
Dative	unc	inc

plural

	1st person	*2nd person*	*3rd person*
Nominative	wē	ġē	hīe, hī, hēo
Accusative	ūs	ēow	hīe, hī, hēo
Genitive	ūre, ūser	ēower	hira, heora
Dative	ūs	ēow	him

You have not previously encountered the dual forms. Meaning roughly "the two of us" and "the two of you," they were probably most often used in Anglo-Saxon life when a romantic or marital couple was being spoken to or when a member of such a couple was speaking. For example, God addresses Adam and Eve in *Genesis* using the second person dual pronoun, and they reply using the first person dual.

Some but not all of the spelling variations that can be encountered in texts are listed in the paradigms. Any form with an **i** will also be found with a **y** in the same place. All of the plural forms spelled **hīe** are also frequently spelled **hīġ**.

Genitive Pronouns and Possessive Adjectives

As in modern English noun phrases such as "my old ring," Old English had possessives that were used essentially as adjectives, and these are in fact called possessive adjectives. They are formed from the genitive case of the corresponding personal pronoun, so that (for example) the dative singular masculine form of **mīn** would be used to modify a dative singular masculine noun: **mīnum ealdan bēage**. Notice that the case of the possessive adjective and its gender depend on the noun modified, not on the gender of the person to whom the pronoun refers: a female speaker would use the masculine dative form in this phrase just as a male speaker would. In general, the third person pronouns do not form possessive adjectives, and the plain form of the genitive personal pronoun is used instead (for example, **his ealdan bēage**). The possessive adjectives have endings that look a bit like the endings of the corresponding personal pronouns, though in fact these are the strong adjective endings, which you will meet in Chapter 10. The singular forms of **mīn** look like this:

	Masculine	*Feminine*	*Neuter*
Nominative	**mīn**	**mīn**	**mīn**
Accusative	**mīnne**	**mīne**	**mīn**
Genitive	**mīnes**	**mīnre**	**mīnes**
Dative	**mīnum**	**mīnre**	**mīnum**

Note especially the ending **-um** for dative singular masculine and neuter. Everywhere else we have met this ending it has signified dative plural, so you will need to be extra careful when you come across this ending on a possessive adjective (or other strong declension adjective) to check the form of the noun it modifies, and conclude that you are dealing with a dative plural only if the ending of the noun is also **-um**.

EXERCISE 8A:
Choose one of the verbs in the table that represents the seven classes of strong verbs. Construct your own table showing the full conjugation of that verb, using the verb **helpan** and its distribution of the five vowels as a model. For example, if you were to choose **beran** to use in this exercise, you would use the vowel of the infinitive in the present indicative (except for second and third persons singular) and present subjunctive, and in the imperative and

present participle. You would use the vowel of the third person singular present indicative (**birð** in the table) in the second and third persons singular of the present indicative. In the preterite (past) tense, you would use **bær** from the table for the first and third persons singular, and the vowel of **bǣron** from the table would fill out the rest of the preterite, including the subjunctive. Finally, you would add the past participle, which appears separately in the table.

EXERCISE 8B:

Translate the following sentences into modern English:

1. Iċ lufie hine.
2. Hē ġeaf hire bēag.
3. Hīe lufodon hīe.
4. Wē ġeafon him stānas.
5. Ġit lufodon hire bearn.
6. Hēo hæfþ ēowre brȳde.
7. Is þæt wīf ūre cwēn?
8. Iċ lufie mīne ġeongan brȳd.
9. Ġē ġeafon hire mīnne ealdan bēag.
10. Ēow ġeaf hēo bēagas.

EXERCISE 8C:

Make five Old English sentences using personal pronouns in cases other than the nominative and/or possessive adjectives, using at least five different persons and numbers for these.

Chapter 9
Weak Nouns and Noun Oddities; Numerals

◆

The strong noun declensions account for most of the nouns you will encounter in Old English, but some commonly occurring nouns are declined differently. These include weak nouns, nouns that change their vowel like modern English mouse/mice, and family terms. This chapter introduces these common exceptions to the standard strong noun declensions. Once you have become acquainted with the noun varieties presented here, there are very few Old English nouns whose workings you will not understand.

Weak Nouns

There are large numbers of weak masculine nouns, quite a few weak feminine nouns, and only really two weak neuter nouns (the words for eye and ear). Weak nouns are pretty easy to learn, because essentially there are not three different declensions here, but one declension with three minor variations. Compare the following three paradigms and you will see why it is possible to say so:

Weak Masculine Noun
hunta (hunter)

	Singular	*Plural*
Nominative	**hunta**	**huntan**
Accusative	**huntan**	**huntan**
Genitive	**huntan**	**huntena**
Dative	**huntan**	**huntum**

71

Weak Neuter Noun
ēage (eye)

	Singular	*Plural*
Nominative	**ēage**	**ēagan**
Accusative	**ēage**	**ēagan**
Genitive	**ēagan**	**ēagena**
Dative	**ēagan**	**ēagum**

Weak Feminine Noun
hearpe (harp)

	Singular	*Plural*
Nominative	**hearpe**	**hearpan**
Accusative	**hearpan**	**hearpan**
Genitive	**hearpan**	**hearpena**
Dative	**hearpan**	**hearpum**

Note that the only differences between the three genders are the form of the nominative singular and (for the neuter) the accusative singular. Note also how much of the paradigm in each case is filled out with the ending **-an**. These declensions are called "weak" because they have so very few changes of ending. This is what makes them so easy to learn, but because the ending **-an** is so ambiguous, it can sometimes be challenging to work out in reading a text what role a particular weak noun is playing in a phrase or sentence.

Some variations you should be aware of:
a) the **-ena** ending of the genitive plural sometimes gets shortened to **-na**, particularly in poetry.
b) the dative plural ending **-um** is if anything even more likely to appear as **-an** or **-on** than in the case of the strong nouns.

Nouns That Change Their Vowel

Some very common Old English nouns change their vowel for the plural, as do **mouse/mice**, **foot/feet**, and **man/men** in modern English. A slight difference in Old English is that the altered vowel usually also appears in the dative singular, and does not appear in the genitive or dative plurals. Two common vowel-changing nouns (often called i-mutated nouns for historical reasons) are **mann** (man, person) and **burg** (city, town, castle):

masculine
mann

	Singular	Plural
Nominative	mann	menn
Accusative	mann	menn
Genitive	mannes	manna
Dative	menn	mannum

(In this very common word, variations abound: nominative and accusative singular can be **man, mon,** or **monn**; nominative and accusative plural can be **men,** as can dative singular; genitive plural can be **monna**; and dative plural **monnum**.)

feminine
burg or **burh**

	Singular	Plural
Nominative	burg	byr(i)ġ
Accusative	burg	byr(i)ġ
Genitive	byr(i)ġ	burga
Dative	byr(i)ġ	burgum

There are rather few vowel-changing masculine nouns (**fōt/fēt** and **tōð/tēð** are common and you should be able to work out what they mean), and no neuter nouns of this type, but there are quite a few feminine ones, including some that have since become regular nouns (that is, they no longer change their vowel for the plural) in modern English:

Singular	Plural
āc (oak)	ǣċ
bōc (book)	bēċ
gāt (goat)	gǣt
gōs (goose)	gēs
lūs (louse)	lȳs
mūs (mouse)	mȳs

Family Terms

The words for father, mother, brother, sister, daughter, and son are frequently encountered and do not follow any of the standard paradigms. They are declined as follows:

masculine
fæder (father)

	Singular	Plural
Nominative	fæder	fæderas
Accusative	fæder	fæderas
Genitive	fæder	fædera
Dative	fæder	fæderum

feminine
mōdor (mother)

	Singular	Plural
Nominative	mōdor	mōdra
Accusative	mōdor	mōdra
Genitive	mōdor	mōdra
Dative	mēder	mōdrum

masculine
brōðor (brother)

	Singular	Plural
Nominative	brōðor	brōðor, brōðra
Accusative	brōðor	brōðor, brōðra
Genitive	brōðor	brōðra
Dative	brēðer	brōðrum

feminine
sweostor; also **swustor, swostor,** etc. (sister)

	Singular	Plural
Nominative	sweostor	sweostor, sweostra
Accusative	sweostor	sweostor, sweostra
Genitive	sweostor	sweostra
Dative	sweostor	sweostrum

feminine
dohtor (daughter)

	Singular	Plural
Nominative	dohtor	dohtor
Accusative	dohtor	dohtor
Genitive	dohtor	dohtra
Dative	dehter	dohtrum

masculine
sunu (son)

	Singular	Plural
Nominative	**sunu**	**suna**
Accusative	**sunu**	**suna**
Genitive	**suna**	**suna**
Dative	**suna**	**sunum**

Numerals

There is little point for the beginning student in memorizing the forms of the Old English numbers, but you might be interested in the system of numbers itself and in its differences and similarities when compared to modern English. Here are the numbers up to twenty (where there are three forms, these are masculine, feminine, and neuter):

one	**ān**
two	**twēġen, twā, tū**
three	**þrīe, þrēo, þrēo**
four	**fēower**
five	**fīf**
six	**siex**
seven	**seofan**
eight	**eahta**
nine	**nigon**
ten	**tīen**
eleven	**endleofan**
twelve	**twelf**
thirteen	**þrēotīene**
fourteen	**fēowertīene**
fifteen	**fīftīene**
sixteen	**sixtīene**
seventeen	**seofontīene**
eighteen	**eahtatīene**
nineteen	**nigontīene**
twenty	**twēntiġ**

After twenty, the tens are predictable and similar to the teens until seventy (**hundseofontiġ**), eighty (**hundeahtatiġ**), ninety (**hundnigontiġ**), and one hundred (**hundtēontiġ**), which is also **hund** and **hundred**. Numbers between the tens themselves are formed by adding the ones at the beginning (**seofon and twēntiġ** is 27), and hundreds come first (**hund and seofon and twēntiġ** is 127), although large and complex numbers are usually written in Roman numerals rather than written out in words, so we do not have as much evidence about them as we might like.

EXERCISE 9A:
Construct paradigms for each of the weak nouns **hunta**, **ēage**, and **hearpe**, in which you add the appropriate demonstratives. Where does doing this remove ambiguity, and where are there still forms that could represent more than one case or more than one number?

EXERCISE 9B:
Read, translate, and solve the following Old English riddle:

> Wer sæt æt wīne mid his wīfum twām
> and his twēġen suna ond his twā dohtor,
> swase sweostor, ond hyra suna twēġen,
> frēolicu frumbearn. Fæder wæs þær inne
> þāra æþelinga ǣġhwæðres mid,
> ēam ond nefa. Ealra wæ̆ron fīfe
> eorla ond īdesa insittendra.

Vocabulary:

wer: man
sæt: sat
wīn (str neut noun): wine
twām (fem dat): two
swas: dear, beloved (**swase** nom pl fem)
frēolic: noble (**frēolicu** nom pl neut)
frumbearn (str neut noun): firstborn child
þær (adv): there
inne (adv): within
æþeling (str masc noun): nobleman
ǣġhwæðer (pron): each (**ǣġhwæðres** gen sing)

ealra (adv): in all
fīfe (nom pl): five
īdes (str fem noun): woman, lady
insittende: sitting inside (**insittendra** gen pl)

EXERCISE 9C:
You guessed it, it seems there are sisters and brothers, mothers and fathers, hunters and their sons and daughters. They live in cities and have eyes. Make five sentences about them. In Old English. Throw in some personal pronouns and some demonstratives to make it interesting.

Chapter 10
Adjectives

◆

Old English adjectives have inflectional endings that depend on the case, number, and gender of the noun they modify. There are two different declensions of adjectives, called the "strong" and the "weak" declensions. Except in poetry, the weak declension is used when the noun is also modified by a demonstrative or possessive, and the strong declension is used when the adjective occurs by itself or when it modifies a noun that does not have a demonstrative or possessive. (In poetry, weak declension adjectives are also used when they modify a noun by themselves or occur alone.)

Weak:
Se **gōda** cyning rīcsode þritiġ ġēara.
　　(The **good** king ruled thirty years.)
Mīn **lēofa** fæder!
　　(My **dear** father!)

Strong:
Þæt wæs **gōd** cyning.
　　(That was a **good** king.)
Hē ne meahte hatian þone hilderinc, þēah hē him **lēof** ne wæs.
　　(He could not hate the warrior, though he was not **dear** to him.)

Strong and Weak Adjective Declensions

The strong and weak adjective declensions are as follows (the adjective in the paradigm means "good"):

Strong:

	Masculine	Neuter	Feminine
Singular			
Nominative	gōd	gōd	gōd
Accusative	gōdne	god	gōde
Genitive	gōdes	gōdes	gōdre
Dative	gōdum	gōdum	gōdre
Plural			
Nominative	gōde	gōd	gōde
Accusative	gōde	gōd	gōde
Genitive	gōdra	gōdra	gōdra
Dative	gōdum	gōdum	gōdum

Weak:

	Masculine	Neuter	Feminine
Singular			
Nominative	gōda	gōde	gōde
Accusative	gōdan	gōde	gōdan
Genitive	gōdan	gōdan	gōdan
Dative	gōdan	gōdan	gōdan
Plural			
Nominative	gōdan	gōdan	gōdan
Accusative	gōdan	gōdan	gōdan
Genitive	gōdra	gōdra	gōdra
Dative	gōdum	gōdum	gōdum

There are some variations of which you should be aware:
a) a certain number of adjectives have an -e ending in the nominative singular of the strong declension, which is dropped before other endings are added.
b) some adjectives have a -u ending in the nominative singular feminine and the nominative and accusative plural neuter of the strong declension.
c) the ending -um for masculine/neuter dative singular and for dative plural (all genders) is especially likely to appear as -an in adjectives.
d) adjectives with two syllables often drop the second syllable for some parts of the paradigm: for example hāliġ becomes hālgum in dative singular masculine.

e) the instrumental ending **-e** appears occasionally, in the masculine and neuter singular strong declensions, modifying a noun in the dative singular.

f) the ending **-ena** sometimes appears instead of **-ra** in the genitive plural of the weak declension.

Comparison of Adjectives

The *comparative* and *superlative* forms of adjectives (the **-er** and **-est** forms of modern English, as in taller, tallest), are formed by the addition of **-ra** and **-ost** endings, so **hwīt** (white) becomes **hwītra** (whiter) and **hwītost** (whitest), **beorht** (bright) becomes **beorhtra** and **beorhtost**, and so on. For the vast majority of adjectives, this addition of endings is the only change, but a few very common adjectives change their vowel in the comparative and superlative:

eald (old)	**yldra**	**yldost**
ġeong (young)	**ġingra**	**ġingest**
hēah (high)	**hīera**	**hīehst**
lang (long)	**lengra**	**lengst**

And some adjectives, most of which are familiar from modern English, have a completely different form for the comparative and superlative:

gōd (good)	**betera**	**betst**
yfel (bad, evil)	**wyrsa**	**wyrst**
miċel (big)	**māra**	**mǣst**
lytel (little, small)	**lǣssa**	**lǣst**

Comparative adjectives are always declined using the weak adjective endings. Superlative adjectives can be declined using either the weak or the strong adjective endings, but in fact are most usually found without any ending in sentences such as **Hē wæs manna mildost** (He was the mildest [i.e., kindest] of men).

Adjectives That Act as Nouns

Old English adjectives are very frequently used as if they were nouns. For example, from the adjective **mǣre** (famous) a noun phrase like **se mǣra** (the famous) can be built (here using the nominative singular masculine form of the weak declension of adjectives). This then can be the subject of a sentence, as in **Se mǣra mynte flēon** (literally, "the famous intended to flee"), a sentence from *Beowulf* which we need to understand as something along the lines of "the famous **one** intended to flee." Note that we do use adjectives like nouns in modern English, but usually with a plural meaning: "The goal of this organization is to house **the homeless** and feed **the hungry**." However, Old English allows a singular adjective use that is impossible in modern English: "***The homeless** was standing on the corner and asked me for spare change."

Some Old English adjectives acquire new meanings as nouns. For example, the adjective **gram** (angry, hostile) in the noun phrase **se grama** (literally, "the angry/hostile [one]") came to mean "the enemy" and specifically "the Devil." Similarly, the comparative adjective **hēahra**, **hēarra** (higher) takes on the particular noun meaning of a superior, lord, or boss, and the comparative adjective **ġingra** (younger) comes to mean an inferior or subordinate when used as a noun.

The þes-Demonstrative

We have already seen that possessive adjectives are declined like strong adjectives. A few other kinds of words use or approximate the endings of the strong declension of adjectives, including the demonstrative **þes** (this/these):

	Masculine	*Neuter*	*Feminine*
Singular			
Nominative	**þes, þæs**	**þis**	**þēos**
Accusative	**þisne**	**þis**	**þās, þisse**
Genitive	**þisses**	**þisses**	**þisse, þissere**
Dative	**þissum**	**þissum**	**þisse, þissere**
Plural			
Nominative	**þās**	**þās**	**þās**
Accusative	**þās**	**þās**	**þās**
Genitive	**þissa**	**þissa**	**þissa**
Dative	**þissum**	**þissum**	**þissum**

The endings here can also be compared to those of the **se**-demonstrative, which in previous chapters were presented separately for masculine, feminine, and neuter, in tables along with the strong noun paradigms:

	Masculine	Neuter	Feminine
Singular			
Nominative	se	þæt	sēo
Accusative	þone	þæt	þā
Genitive	þæs	þæs	þǣre
Dative	þǣm, þām	þǣm, þām	þǣre
Plural			
Nominative	þā	þā	þā
Accusative	þā	þā	þā
Genitive	þāra	þāra	þāra
Dative	þǣm, þām	þǣm, þām	þǣm, þām

Who? Why?

Old English *interrogative pronouns* were used for asking questions in much the same way as modern English **who** and **what**.

Hwa meahte mē swelc ġewit ġifan? (Who might give me such wisdom?)
Hwa sæde þē þæt þū nacod wǣre? (Who told you that you were naked?)
Hwæt is se ġewuldroda cyning? (What is that glorified king?)
Hwæs hunta eart þū? (Whose hunter are you?)

The full declension looks like this:

	Masculine	Neuter	Feminine
Nominative	hwa	hwa	hwæt
Accusative	hwone	hwone	hwæt
Genitive	hwæs	hwæs	hwæs
Dative	hwǣm, hwām	hwǣm, hwām	hwǣm, hwām

There is also an instrumental form **hwȳ**, but this does not usually mean as expected "by means of what?", but rather "why?" (Similarly, the instrumental demonstrative pronoun **þȳ** is very often to be translated "therefore, for that reason" rather than "by means of that.")

Hwȳ didest þū þæt?
(Why did you do that?)
Drihten cwæð to him, "Hwȳ eart ðū yrre?"
(The Lord said to him, "Why are you angry?")

The interrogative pronouns can also be used as indefinite pronouns:

Men ne cunnon secgan tō sōðe **hwā** þæm hlæste onfeng.
(Men cannot say truly **who** received that cargo.)

EXERCISE 10A:
Choose three nouns (you now know many), one for each of the three genders, and make two tables for each of them, one showing them with strong declension adjectives, one showing them with **þes**-demonstratives and weak-declension adjectives. In addition to **gōd**, you could use any of the following adjectives: **beorht** (bright), **milde** (kind, generous), **hāt** (hot, exciting), **seldcūð** (unusual, strange), **rēðe** (cruel, terrible), **rīce** (rich, powerful), **yfel** (bad, evil). Note that adjectives that end in -e drop that ending before adding the other endings (so **mildum**, not *mildeum*).

EXERCISE 10B:
Translate each of the following expressions into Old English using the case indicated:
1. this generous bishop (genitive)
2. the cruel king (accusative)
3. an unusual ring (dative)
4. unusual rings (accusative)
5. a good man (accusative)
6. powerful kings (genitive)
7. the evil woman (nominative)
8. bright cities (dative)
9. these evil sons (nominative)
10. whose bright ring? (nominative)

EXERCISE 10C:
Create three Old English questions from the text you are currently reading. For example, from the Abraham and Isaac story sentence, "God wolde þā

fandian Abrahames ġehiersumnesse" (God wanted then to test Abraham's obedience), you could make either

> Hwa wolde fandian Abrahames ġehiersumnesse?
> (Who wanted to test Abraham's obedience?)
> or
> Hwæs ġehiersumnesse wolde God fandian?
> (Whose obedience did God want to test?)

Chapter II
Word Order in Noun Phrases and Sentences; the Subjunctive

◆

In general, Old English word order is often remarkably similar to modern English, but there are differences that make rather unsuccessful the translation strategy of looking up each word in a text and writing the glossary definition above the word without worrying about things like cases, at least part of the time. In this chapter we look at some of the similarities and differences between modern English and Old English syntax (word order) as found in phrases and sentences, and also examine the subjunctive mood a bit more carefully.

The Noun Phrase

The average Old English noun phrase, especially in prose, looks a lot like a modern English noun phrase:

determiner	adjective(s)	noun
the	old	men
my	big fat	wedding
se	ēadiga	arcebisceop
	(blessed)	(archbishop)
ūre	gōda heofonlica	fæder
	(good heavenly)	

You need to be careful, though, to watch out for situations where these elements either do not come in the order you expect them to or appear in sequences that are illegal in modern English. For example, an adjective does not necessarily come before the noun it modifies, and two adjectives modifying the same noun can even come on either side of the noun:

> Sidroc eorl se ġeonga
>   (Earl Sidroc the young; the young earl Sidroc)
> tamra dēora unbebohtra syx hund
>   (six hundred [of] tame, unsold animals)
> berenne kyrtel oðð e yterenne
>   (a bearskin or otterskin kirtle/coat)

Likewise, a possessive may come after the noun it modifies, particularly in direct address:

> Fæder mīn, iċ ascie hwær seo offrung sīe.
>   (My father, I ask where the offering may be.)
> Fæder ūre, þū þe eart in heofonum, ...
>   (Our Father, you who art in Heaven, ...)

And where modern English allows only one determiner (possessives and articles are the main determiners), Old English permits both a possessive and a demonstrative:

> his þā æfæstan tungan
>   (his the pious tongue [that pious tongue of his])
> hæleð mīn se lēofa
>   (man my the dear [my dear man])

When a compound noun phrase, that is, one with two or more nouns linked with "and," is the subject of a sentence, the first noun may precede the verb and the others follow:

> Cynewulf benam Siġebryht his rīċes **and West Seaxna wiotan**.
>   (Cynewulf **and the council of the West Saxons** deprived
>   Sigebryht of his kingdom.)

Note that the verb **benam** here is singular, even though the entire compound subject is plural, because the verb responds only to whatever element of the compound subject precedes it, not to the whole subject.

Word Order in the Sentence: SVO, SOV, OSV, VSO?

Old English sentence structure, despite the freedom granted by the case system to use unusual word orders for emphasis, usually follows predictable patterns. Sometimes these patterns are familiar to us—after all, Old English gradually evolved into Middle English and then into modern English, so we have a right to expect some similarities. Other structures are not so familiar.

Linguists often use the shorthand S (subject), O (object or object-like things), and V (verb), when talking about standard sequences of these elements in forming a sentence in a particular language. In these terms, modern English is an SVO language: it has a strong preference for sentences that start with a subject, follow that with the verb, and conclude with the object or other elements of the preterite. Old English was also an SVO language for direct statements, but the preference was not as strong as in modern English, and other orders were possible or even more common in particular circumstances. This means that the student of Old English needs to be attuned to the possibility of (especially) an object coming where she or he expects a subject, and vice versa.

SVO Order
    Hēo (S) cende (V) hyre frumcennedan sunu (O).
      (She gave birth to her first-born son.)
    And hīġ (S) efstende cōmon and ġemetton (V) Marrian and Iosep and
    þæt ċild on binne alēd (O).
      (And they hurrying came and met Mary and Joseph and the child
      laid in the manger.)
    God (S) wolde fandian (V) Abrahames ġehiersumnesse (O), and
    clipode (V) his naman (O).
      (God wanted to test Abraham's obedience and called his name.)

SOV: This order appears frequently without any apparent reason other than (possibly) emphasis, but it is particularly common when the object is a pronoun and in subordinate clauses:

SOV Order:

for emphasis?
Hē (S) þær wēofod (O) arǣrde (V) on þā ealdan wīsan, and þone wudu
(O) ġelōgode (V)
(He there raised up an altar in the old manner and arranged the
wood.)

with pronoun object
hēo (S) hine (O) mid ċildclāþum bewand (V) and hine (O) on binne
alēde (V)
(she wrapped him in swaddling-clothes and laid him in a manger)
... iċ (S) þē (O) nū bletsie (V) ...
(I now bless you)

in a subordinate clause
Mid þȳ þe se cyning (S) þæt (O) ġeseah (V) ...
(When the king saw that ...)

VSO: A subject following the verb immediately, with the object (or object-
like element) at the end, is a normal way to ask a question. It is also a precious
key to the dilemma facing the beginning translator when she or he is trying to
figure out sentences with *correlating conjunctions*, namely how to decide
which of the clauses is subordinate and which is the main clause.

Correlating conjunctions join clauses together by adding a word or words
to each of the clauses, which work together to do the joining. Typical examples in modern English do not involve subordination: "**Not only** did I steal her
cake recipe, **but also** I copied her dinner plan." Old English, however, has a
variety of correlating conjunctions that do involve subordination, of which the
ones that come up most often are **þā ... þā ...** (when ... then ...), **þær ... þær ...**
(where ... there...), and **þonne ... þonne ...** (when ... then ...). These are particularly maddening to the beginning reader because each clause is introduced
by the same word, yet only one of the clauses specifies the main idea of the
sentence. Context can be helpful, but the almost perfect secret to sorting out
this kind of sentence is word order: the clause with SVO order (normal
English word order) or SOV order is subordinate, and the clause with VSO
order is the main clause, almost all the time. (Some writers give an additional
clue by doubling the introductory word in the subordinate clause, so if you
have **þā þā ... þā ...**, you know that the clause introduced by **þā þā ...** is the
subordinate clause.)

VSO Order:

in questions

Hæfst (V) þū (S) æniġne ġefēran (O)?
(Do you have any companion?)
Wǣre (V) þū (S) tōdæġ on huntnoþe (O)?
(Were you out hunting today?)

in subordinate clauses

Þā se cyning (S) þā þās word (O) ġehyrde (V), þā andswarode (V)
hē (S) him (O).
(When the king then heard these words, then he answered him.)
Þā ðæt folc (S) hine (O) þā ġeseah (V) swā ġescyrpedne, þā wēndon
(V) hēo (S) þæt he wedde (O).
(When the people then saw him so decked out, then they believed
that he was mad.)
Þonne hē (S) ġeseah (V) þā hearpan (O) him nēalēcan, þonne ārās (V)
hē (S).
(When he saw the harp approaching him, then he got up.)

The Subjunctive Mood

The subjunctive mood was introduced briefly in Chapter 6 as governing the
verb when in some way its action is conceived of as unreal: the object, for
example, of a wish, command, fear, conjecture, belief, or hypothesis. The subjunctive has almost disappeared from modern English, so a few examples of
usage are offered here in an attempt to complete the picture.

1. The subjunctive is often used for reported speech:

Hē cwæþ þæt he **būde** on þǣm lande norþweardum wiþ þā Westsǣ.
(He said that he **lived** in the land northward along the West Sea.)
Hē sæde ðæt Norðmanna land **wǣre** swȳþe lang.
(He said that the land of the Northmen **was** very long.)
Þā gyt hē frǣġn, hū nēah þǣre tīde **wǣre** ...
(Again he asked, how near to the time it **was** ...)

2. The subjunctive is used for advice, wishes, and commands:

> Gode ælmihtegum **sīe** ðonc.
> (Thanks **be** to God Almighty.)
> Hēo hine þā monade and lærde þæt he ... munuchād **onfenge**.
> (She then admonished and advised him that he **receive** monkhood.)
> Mē ðyncð betre, ġif iow swæ ðyncð, ðæt wē ēac sume bēċ ... **wenden**.
> (It seems better to me, if it seems so to you, that we also **translate** some books.)
> Iċ nū lǣre þæt wē þā hraþe fȳre **forbærnen**.
> (I now advise that we quickly **burn them down** with fire.)

3. The subjunctive is used where the action of the verb is unrealized, because it refers to a future time, a purpose, a conjecture, something avoided, or a hypothetical situation:

> Uncūð hū longe ðær swǣ ġelǣrede biscepas **sīen**.
> ([It is] unknown how long bishops so learned **will be** there.)
> ... ǣr ðǣm ðe hit eall forhergod **wǣre** ...
> (Before it **was** [to be] all destroyed by war.)
> Hē ġeband þā his sunu, and his sweord ātēah, þæt hē hine **ġeoffrode**.
> (He bound his son then, and picked up his sword, that he **might offer** him.)
> Iċ wēne ðætte nōht moniġe beġiondan Humbre **nǣren**.
> (I expect that there **were not** many beyond the Humber.)
> Þȳ læs wulfas **forswelġen** hīe.
> (Lest wolves **swallow** them up.)
> Swelce hīe **cwǣden** ...
> (As if they **said** ...)
> Swylc swā þū æt swǣsendum **sitte** mid þīnum ealdormannum ...
> (As if you **were to sit** at the feast with your nobles ...)

Subjunctives and Participles of bēon and habban

The subjunctives and participles of the verbs **bēon** and **habban** were omitted when these verbs were introduced in Chapter 5. They are as follows:

bēon

	singular (all persons)	*plural (all persons)*
subjunctive present	**sīe, bēo**	**sīen, bēon**
subjunctive preterite	**wǣre**	**wǣren**

present participle
  wesende
past participle
  (ġe)bēon

habban

	singular (all persons)	*preterite (all persons)*
subjunctive present	**hæbbe**	**hæbben**
subjunctive preterite	**hæfde**	**hæfden**

present participle
  hæbbende
past participle
  (ġe)hæfd

EXERCISE II A:
Take from your readings or compose yourself five simple Old English sentences that have bēon or habban as their main verb. Preface them with "Iċ wēne þæt" and convert the verbs to subjunctives.

EXERCISE II B:
Analyze the paradigms for strong and weak verbs given in Chapters 6 and 8 and the paradigms of **bēon** and **habban**. At what points is the subjunctive of each of these verbs distinct from the indicative? In what places is it identical?

EXERCISE II C:
Choose three sentences from your current Old English reading and conduct an SVO analysis, finding the subject of each verb and marking it with S, and so on. What orders of sentence constituents do you find?

Chapter 12
Old English Metre, Poetic Diction, and Poetic Syntax

◆

Old English poetry used alliteration as its main poetic technique, in a fairly short poetic line divided into two half-lines that shared alliteration and that had to conform to particular metrical patterns. Rhyme was only occasionally exploited. The demands of alliteration fostered the development and maintenance of a distinctive poetical vocabulary, so that many of the words in our surviving corpus of Old English texts survive only or primarily in poetry. The alliterative metre also imposed demands on poets that tended to distort the normal syntax of prose as discussed in Chapter 11. Moreover, particular kinds of repetition, including noun-phrase and verb apposition, were highly valued as decorative effects in poetry. All of these factors impose additional interpretive burdens on the reader of Old English poetry, so they will receive special (though necessarily brief) treatment here.

Old English Metre

The Old English poetic line was composed of two "half-lines," normally separated from one another by white space in printed editions (and sometimes punctuated with an elevated dot in Anglo-Saxon manuscripts). The half-lines were only occasionally, and then as a kind of extra fancy patterning, connected with rhyme. Rather, alliteration, that is, matching initial sounds of stressed syllables, was the connector:

> Nū sculon **her**igean   **Heo**fonrīces weard,
> **Meo**tudes **meaht**   ond his **mōd**ġeþanc,
> **weorc wul**dorfæder   swa hē **wun**dra ġehwæs
> **eċe** drihten   ōr onstealde.

From the sample above (the first four lines of Caedmon's Hymn), the basic principles can be derived. Each line alliterates on a different sound, either a consonant or a vowel (in which case any vowel alliterates with any other vowel). There is at least one alliterating syllable in each half-line. Usually the second half-line has only one alliterating syllable: it will be the first strongly stressed syllable in the half-line. One or two syllables of the first half-line will alliterate with that key syllable in the second half-line, producing the following possible alliteration patterns:

A A | A x   (lines 2 and 3 above)
A x | A x   (line 4 above)
x A | A x   (line 1 above)

(Capital A represents a strongly stressed syllable that alliterates; small x represents a strongly stressed syllable that does not alliterate.)

Important additional rules governing alliteration are that words beginning with **sp** alliterate only with **sp**, not with words beginning with **s** alone or with words beginning with **sc** or **st**; similarly for **sc** and **st**, which alliterate with **sc** and **st** only; and, for most poems, **ġ** alliterates with **g**, and **ċ** alliterates with **c**. A strongly stressed syllable (also called a "lift") does not need to be the first syllable in a word to alliterate, so weakly stressed prefixes do not interfere with the alliteration of the following strongly stressed syllable.

In addition to alliteration, the half-lines of Old English poetry are perceived as poetry rather than prose because they conform to a very small set of rhythmical patterns, first identified by Eduard Sievers in the nineteenth century, and thus called Sievers' Five Types. (Although a variety of explanations for the specific requirements of Old English metre have been proposed since Sievers, his Five Types are commonly used by Old English specialists to this day.) Unlike the metres of later English verse, these patterns do not rigorously determine the number of syllables in a half-line, in which there can be substantial variation. Rather, they specify the relation between the strongly stressed syllables and syllables receiving lesser stress. The five basic patterns are as follows:

Type A: falling-falling; or strong, weak, strong, weak (/ x / x)

               brocen **wurd**e

               ... **hors** forlætan,

               fēor āfȳsan ...

Type A is the most common half-line form in Old English verse. There can be as many as five weakly stressed syllables between the first lift and the second lift.

Type B: rising-rising; or weak, strong, weak, strong (x / x /)

               Þā þæt **Off**an **mæg** ...

               ... and tō þære **hilde stōp**.

Type B verses can have up to five weakly stressed syllables preceding the first lift, and up to two (but no more) between the first and second lifts.

Type C: clashing; or weak, strong, strong, weak (x / / x)

               þæt se **cniht nold**e ...

               ... ongan þa **forð ber**an

Type C verses can have up to six weakly stressed syllables preceding the first lift. The second lift can be a syllable with a short vowel.

Type D: strong and then falling; or strong, strong, half-strong, weak OR strong, strong, weak, half-strong (/ / \ x OR / / x \ )

               grim gūð_pleg_a

               brimliþen_dra_

(Secondary stress is marked with italics.) Type D verses can have up to three additional weakly stressed syllables separating the two lifts with which the verse begins.

Type E: falling-rising; strong, half-strong, weak, strong (/ \ x /)

               wand _wac_ne **æsc**

               æt_tryn_e **ord**

Type E permits the least variation in number of syllables: one additional weakly stressed syllable may precede the final lift.

Poetic Diction

The need to alliterate in order to join each pair of half-lines, in addition to the limitations on the acceptable metrical form of the half-line discussed above, put a heavy premium on vocabulary in the poetry of the Old English period. In particular, in order to avoid local repetition of words (one of the fundamental principles of pre-twentieth century poetry of all kinds, and particularly of Old English poetry) and in order to vary the alliterating consonant (a particular requirement of alliterative verse), poets needed a stock of words with different alliterating sounds for frequently occurring concepts such as (in heroic poetry) lords and rulers, men, and weapons, and (for religious poetry) God, salvation, and Heaven. It also seems to have been the case that poems and their vocabulary were remembered and passed down orally from generation to generation in Anglo-Saxon society, perhaps even after the introduction of writing. The combination of these two factors, the particular demands of alliterative verse and the persistence of poetic vocabulary through time—in some cases past the point when a particular word had stopped being used in daily speech—meant that Old English developed a large stock of poetic vocabulary, words that we find exclusively or almost exclusively in poetry.

For example, in the following list of words that mean roughly "man," though sometimes with an additional meaning such as "warrior" or "hero," the words in bold are found mostly or entirely in verse:

> æþele, **beorn**, ċēorl, **drihtguma**, eorl, esne, **fīras** (plural), **folcwer**, **freca**, frēomann, **guma**, gummann, **gumrinc**, **hæle**, **hæleð**, hīred-mann, lēod, **lēodwer**, **mago**, **magorinc**, mann, manna, **mæcg**, rinc, scealc, **searohabbend**, **secg**, **selesecg**, **sweordbora**, **sweordfreca**, þeġn, **þēodguma**, wæpnedmann, wer

Notice also how many of the words in the above list are compound nouns. For example, we have **mago, rinc**, and also **magorinc; mann, guma**, and also **gummann** (plus **gumrinc**!); **lēod, wer, lēodwer**, and also **folcwer** (man "of the people"). Compound nouns are very frequent throughout the extant corpus of Old English, but the demands of creating alliterative verse are no doubt responsible for the fact that many compounds that occur in poetry are found only in poetry. This could mean either that the compounds that were used in poetry simply formed part of the specialized poetic diction or (since many such compounds occur in only one place in the entire poetic corpus) that creating new nonce-compounds (compound words created on the spot for a particular occasion) was one of the poetic skills. Our surviving corpus of texts is too small to tell which explanation is more likely, and there is even the possibility that if we had a much expanded library of surviving Old English prose texts we would find a few examples of what now seem to us to be exclusively poetic words in prose as well as in poetry.

The Syntax of Poetry

In the previous chapter we saw that Old English had a standard SVO order which was varied for emphasis or in particular surroundings to other orders. The first thing to say about grammar in Old English poetry is that those other orders of sentence constituents become much more frequent. Things may not be where you expect to find them. This means that you have to be on your toes, and particularly attentive to case as indicated by inflectional endings. Take a look at the first sentence of *Beowulf*:

> Wē Gār-Dena in ġēardagum,/ þēodcyninga þrym ġefrūnon,/ hū ðā æþelingas ellen fremedon.
> (We of the Spear-Danes in olden days, of the kings-of-people power learned, how those noblemen bravery did.)

The literal translation running below the Old English words above shows how necessary it is going to be to apply your knowledge of the Old English case system in order to sort out the meaning of poetry. Start by looking for a subject and a verb: here **wē** is the nominative form and **ġefrūnon** is a plural verb to match it, so there we have the subject and main verb (**þrym** could also be nominative, but it is singular so can't be the subject of the plural verb). **Ġefrūnon** (heard, learned, heard of) needs an object, so **þrym** must be accusative: "we learned of the power." The genitive plurals in that part of the sentence then have to be possessive: "we learned of the power of the Spear-Danes, of the kings-of-people" OR "we learned of the power of the kings-of-people of the Spear-Danes" (depending on whether you take **Gār-Dena** and **þēodcyninga** as parallel expressions for the same folks or as one modifying the other). **In ġēardagum** (in olden days) as a prepositional phrase likely modifies the noun it is closest to, **Gār-Dena**, since presumably the act of hearing, learning, or finding out did not happen in the distant past. Finally, "how those noblemen bravery did" is easy to unravel to "how those noblemen did bravery (i.e., brave deeds)" and must be a parallel object for **ġefrūnon**: "We learned of the power of the kings-of-people of the Spear-Danes in olden days, (we learned) how those noblemen did bravery."

Other special characteristics of word order in poetry you need especially to watch out for:

1) pronoun subjects are frequently omitted if it is clear who the agent is from the context (and sometimes when it isn't clear):

> Ġewāt ðā nēosian, syþðan niht becōm,
> hean hūses, hū hit Hring-Dene
> æfter bēorþeġe ġebūn hæfdon.
> Fand þā ðǣr inne æþelinga ġedriht ...
> > ([He] went then to investigate, after night came,
> > the high house, how the Ring-Danes
> > after beer-drinking had settled in it.
> > [He] found then therein the troop of nobles ...)

Here it can be understood from the context that the monster Grendel is the agent even though he hasn't been mentioned for ten lines, so no subject is supplied for either of the verbs **ġewāt** (went) or **fand** (found).

2) parts of phrases that grammatically belong together may well be separated:

> ... hē dōgora ġehwām **drēam** ġehȳrde
> **hlūdne** in healle.
> > (... he each day heard **loud merriment** in the hall.)

Here **hlūdne** (loud) modifies **drēam** (merriment) despite the fact that there is an intervening word—and there are examples with much more radical separation than this.

3) nouns without demonstratives or possessives may frequently be definite (i.e., you should supply "the" when translating, and not "a" or "an"):

> **Weard** maþelode ðǣr on wicge sæt,
> **ombeht** unforht ...
> > ([The] **guard** spoke, where [he] sat on [his] horse,
> > [the] **officer** unfrightened ...).

Poetic Style, Especially Apposition

Entire books have been written about poetic style in the Old English period, which this short section will not attempt to capture. You will certainly find much to admire and also to wonder at (not necessarily in a positive sense, although maybe) as you begin to read Old English poetry. What is most essential for you to know about style as you begin is an aspect of stylistic expectation that will be liable at first to throw you off, namely that Old English poetry prizes repetition with variation and loves the interlacing of sentence elements. Perhaps first encouraged by the restrictions imposed by alliteration and the rhythmic half-line, these aspects are prominent enough that we have to conclude that they were intentionally sought after. The beginning reader needs to expect them and to realize that the confusion and even despair they bring to the first-time translator would have been a mild and pleasurable exercise of decipherment to the original audience (who knew their cases by heart, if a gentle hint is permitted). The concluding sentence of Caedmon's Hymn, the earliest (roughly) datable Old English poem, already cited at the beginning of this chapter, can serve as an example:

> Þā middanġeard monncynnes Weard,
> ēċe Drihten, æfter tēode
> fīrum foldan, Frēa ælmihtiġ.

In its own order, this can be translated "Then Middle Earth [the] Lord of mankind, [the] eternal Lord afterwards adorned, for men the world, [the] almighty Lord." But note that what is going on in this sentence is that there are three subjects (**monncynnes Weard, ēċe Drihten**, and **Frēa ælmihtiġ**), all of them epithets for God, and two direct objects (**middanġeard, foldan**). Most people will group these in order to translate, "Then the Lord of mankind, the eternal Lord, the mighty Lord, adorned Middle Earth, the world for men," and that is legitimate as a translation tactic, but of course it doesn't get across the confusion entailed in working toward that translation, a confusion caused by the poet's sheer delight in varying the terms for God while repeatedly referring to God and in interweaving the verb and two objects with those terms for God. *Apposition*, as the multiplication of these noun phrases all playing the same grammatical role is called (a prosaic modern English example of apposition occurs in phrases like "my son the doctor"), can also occur with verbs, and you should also be attuned to the possibility that a whole phrase or clause will be repeated but with different vocabulary.

EXERCISE 12A:
Identify the alliterating sound and the syllables that alliterate in each line of the following extract from a poem (*The Battle of Maldon*):

> Mē sendon tō þē sǣmen snelle,
> hēton ðē secgan þæt þū most sendan raðe
> bēagas wið ġebēorġe; and ēow betere is
> þæt ġē þisne gārrǣs mid gafole forġyldon,
> þonne wē swa hearde hilde dǣlon.

(Vigorous seamen sent me to you, commanded [me] to say to you that you must quickly send rings [i.e., treasure] in exchange for protection, and it is better for you that you pay your way out of this battle with tribute than that we share such a hard war.)

EXERCISE 12B:
Identify, for each half-line in the piece of poetry in Exercise 12A, which of the Sievers types it is.

EXERCISE 12C:
A more natural way of phrasing the first line and a half might be "Sǣmen snelle sendon mē tō þē, hēton mē þē secgan...." What changes has the poet made to this normal prose order of words? What specifically has he achieved in terms of metre?

Abraham and Isaac (Genesis 22:1-19)

This and the following biblical passage have facing-page glossaries that have been made simple for beginners to use. The abbreviations used in these early glossaries should be easy for students to work out, but in any case are listed on p. 134.

1 God wolde þā fandian Abrahames ġehīersumnesse, and clipode his naman,

2 and cwæð him ðus tō: "Nim ðīnne āncennedan sunu Isaac, þe ðū lufast, and far tō þām lande *Visionis* hraðe, and ġeoffra hine þǣr uppan ānre dūne."

3 Abraham ðā ārās on þǣre ilcan nihte, and fērde mid twām cnapum tō þām fierlenan lande, and Isaac samod, on assum rīdende.

---

1 Verse numbers are provided for students who would like to compare the Old English version to the Biblical text, but this is not a word-by-word translation; for example, words corresponding to what is numbered as verse 1 here do not occur in the Bible.

2 **cwæð him ðus tō**: "said thus to him"—a preposition can follow its pronoun object in Old English

Abrahames (proper name, masc gen sing): of Abraham; Abraham's
āncennedan (adj, masc acc sing): only begotten
and (conj): and
ānre (adj, dat sing fem): a; one
ārās (str verb, 3rd pers sing pret indic): arose (from ārīsan)
assum (wk masc noun, dat pl): asses; donkeys
clipode (wk verb, 3rd pers sing pret indic): called; cried out; summoned (from clipian)
cnapum (wk masc noun, dat pl): servants
cwæð (str verb, 3rd pers sing pret indic): said (from cweðan)
dūne (str fem noun, dat sing): mountain
fandian (wk verb, infinitive): to test
far (str verb, imper sing): go; travel (from faran)
fērde (wk verb, 3rd pers sing pret indic): went; travelled (from fēran)
fierlenan (adj, dat sing neut): distant; far-off
God (str masc nom sing): God
ġehīersumnesse (noun, fem acc sing): obedience
him (3rd pers pron, masc dat sing): him
hine (3rd pers pron, masc acc sing): him
his (3rd pers pron, masc gen sing): his
hraðe (adverb): quickly
ilcan (adj, dat sing fem): same
Isaac (proper name, masc acc sing): Isaac
lande (str neut noun, dat sing): land
lufast (wk verb, 2nd pers sing pres indic): love (from lufian)
mid (prep w. dat): with
naman (wk masc noun, acc sing): name
nihte (str fem noun, dat sing): night
nim (str verb, imper sing): take (from niman)
ġeoffra (wk verb, imper sing): sacrifice; offer up (from ġeoffrian)
on (prep w. dat): on
rīdende (str verb, pres part): riding (from rīdan)
samod (adv): together; too; at the same time
sunu (noun, masc acc sing): son
þā, ðā (adv): then; when
þǣr (adverb): there
þǣre (dem pron, dat sing fem): the; that
þām (dem pron, dat sing neut): the; that
þe (rel pron): whom; that; which
ðīnne (poss adj, acc sing masc): your
ðū (2nd pers pron, nom sing): thou; you
ðus (adv): thus
tō (prep w. dat): to
twām (num, masc dat): two
uppan (prep w. dat): upon
Visionis (Latin): of vision; of the Vision (from the Hebrew *Moriah*, meaning "vision")
wolde (3rd pers sing pret indic): wanted; desired (from willan)

[handwritten margin note: repetition of — emphasis]

[handwritten: ge = y]

4 Þā on ðone þriddan dæg, þā hīe ðā dūne gesāwon ðǣr ðǣr hīe tō sceoldon tō ofslēanne Isaac,

5 ðā cwæð Abraham tō ðām cnapum þus: "Anbidiað ēow hēr mid þām assum sume hwīle. Iċ and þæt ċild gāð unc tō ġebiddenne, and wē syððan cumað sōna eft tō ēow."

6 Abraham þā hēt Isaac beran þone wudu tō þǣre stōwe, and hē self bær his sweord and fȳr.

[handwritten translation:]

4. Then on the third day, when they the mountain saw where they to had to (where they were supposed to go) to slay Isaac,

5. Then said Abraham to the servants thus: "Wait here with the donkeys some time. I and the child are going to to pray, and we afterwards will come immediately again to you.

6. Abraham then ordered Isaac to bring the wood to the place, and he himself brought his sword and fire

[handwritten: cwþo]

---

4 **ðǣr ðǣr hīe tō sceoldon**: "where they were supposed to go"—verbs of motion are often omitted in Old English

5 **anbidiað ēow**: translate "wait"—the pronoun **ēow** is reflexive and does not need to be translated

gāð unc to ġebiddenne: "are going to pray"—**unc**, which is a dual pronoun (the two of us) is reflexive and does not need to be translated

anbidiað (wk verb, imper pl): wait (from anbidian)

assum (wk masc noun, dat pl): asses; donkeys

bær (str verb, 3rd pers sing pret indic): brought, carried (from beran)'

beran (str verb, infin): to bring, carry

ċild (str neut noun, nom sing): child

cnapum (wk noun, dat pl masc): servants

cumað (str verb, 1st pers pl pres indic): [will] come (from cuman)

cwæð (str verb, 3rd pers sing pret indic): said (from cweðan)

dæġ (str masc noun, acc sing): day

dūne (str fem noun, acc sing): mountain

eft (adv): again, back

ēow (2nd pers pron, dat or acc pl): you

fȳr (str neut noun, acc sing): fire

gāð (anom verb, 1st pers pl pres indic): [will] go; walk (from gan)

hē (3rd pers pron, nom sing): he

hēr (adv): here

hēt (str verb, 3rd pers sing pres indic): ordered (from hātan)

hīe (3rd pers pron, nom pl): they

hwīle (str fem noun, acc sing): time; while

iċ (1st pers pron, nom sing): I

mid (prep w. dat): with

ġesāwon (str verb, 3rd pers pl pret indic): saw (from ġesēon)

sceoldon (wk verb, 3rd pers pl pret indic): must; had to (from sculan)

self (pron): (him)self

sōna (adverb): immediately

stōwe (str fem noun, dat sing): place

sume (adj, acc sing fem): some; a certain

sweord (str neut noun, acc sing): sword

syððan (adv): after; afterwards

ðā (dem pron, acc sing fem): the

þā, ðā (adv): then; when

ðǣr ðǣr (conj): where

þǣre (dem pron, dat sing fem): the; that

þæt (dem pron, nom sing neut): the; that

ðām (dem pron, dat pl): the

ðone, þone (dem pron, acc sing masc): the

þriddan (num, dat sing masc): third

þus (adv): thus, in this way

tō ġebiddene (str verb, inflect infin): to pray (from biddan)

tō ofslēanne (str vb, inflect infin): to slay (from ofslēan)

unc (1st pers dual pron, dative): us two (reflexive)

wē (1st pers pl pron, nom): we

wudu (masc noun, acc sing): wood

eow~ you guys y'all

[handwritten margin note: may be]

7 Isaac ðā āscode Abraham his fæder: "Fæder mīn, iċ āscie hwǣr sēo offrung sīe. Hēr is wudu and fȳr."

8 Him andwyrde se fæder, "God foresċēawað, mīn sunu, him self ðā offrunge."

9 Hīe cōmon þā tō ðǣre stōwe þe him ġesweotolode God, and hē ðǣr wēofod ārǣrde on ðā ealdan wīsan, and þone wudu ġelōgode swā swā hē hit wolde habban tō his suna bærnette syððan he ofslaġen wurde. Hē ġeband þā his sunu,

[handwritten subjunctive note above "wurde"]

[handwritten translation:]

7. Isaac then asked abraham his father: "Father m'y, I ask where the offering may be. Here is wood and fire."

8. To him answered the father. "God will provide, my son, for himself the offering"

9. They came then to that place that [to] him revealed God, and he the altar erected in the old way, and the wood arranged in such a way he it wanted have to his son burning when he would be killed. He bound his son,

which God revealed

just as he wanted to have it, for the burning of his son when he would be killed.

ʳafter he would be slain. *slain*

---

8 **him self**: for himself, to himself

9 **þe him ġesweotolode God**: "which God revealed to him"—**God** is the subject of the verb
 on ðā ealdan wisan: "in the old way," that is, as an altar for animal sacrifice as opposed to a Christian church altar
 syððan he ofslaġen wurde: "when he would be killed"; "after he was killed"

[handwritten note:] sīe - subjunctive - possibility →may

andwyrde (wk verb, 3rd pers sing pret indic): answered (from andwyrdan)
ārǣrde (wk verb, 3rd pers sing pret indic): erected (from ārǣran)
āscie (wk verb, 1st pers sing pres indic): ask (from āscian)
āscode (wk verb, 3rd pers sing pret indic): asked (from āscian)
bærnette (str neut noun, dat sing): burning
ġeband (str verb, 3rd pers sing pres indic): bound (from bindan)
cōmon (str verb, 3rd pers pl pret indic): came (from cuman)
ealdan (adj, acc sing fem): old
fæder (masc noun, nom, acc or dat sing): father
foresċēawað (wk verb, 3rd pers sing pres indic): will provide; will decree (from foresċēawian)
fȳr (str neut noun, nom sing): fire
God (str masc noun, nom sing): God
habban (infin): have
hēr (adverb): here
hīe (3rd pers pron, dat pl): they
him (3rd pers pron, dat sing masc): him, to him
hit (3rd pers pron, acc sing neut): it
hwǣr (adv): where
iċ (1st pers pron, nom sing): I
is (verb, 3rd pers sing pres indic): is (from bēon)
ġelōgode (wk verb, 3rd pers sing pret indic): arranged; put (from (ġe)lōgian)
mīn (1st pers pron, gen sing): my
offrung (str fem noun, nom sing): offering; sacrifice (offrunge acc sing)
ofslaġen (past participle): slayed (from ofslēan)
on (prep w. acc): in
self (pron): self
sēo (dem pron, nom sing fem): the; that
sīe (3rd pers sing pres subj): is; may be (from bēon)
stōwe (str fem noun, dat sing): place
sunu (masc noun, nom sing): son (suna gen sing)
swā swā (conj): as, in such a way as
ġesweotolode (wk verb, 3rd pers sing pret indic): revealed (from (ġe)sweotolian)
syððan (conj): after, when
ðā (dem pron, acc sing fem): the
ðā, þā (adv): then
ðǣr (adv): there
ðǣre (dem pron, dat sing fem): the, that
þe (rel pron): which, that
þone (dem pron, acc sing masc): the
tō (prep w. dat): to, for
wēofod (str neut noun, acc sing): altar
wīsan (wk fem noun, acc sing): way, manner
wolde (wk verb, 3rd pers sing pret indic): wanted
wudu (masc noun, nom/acc sing): wood
wurde (wk verb, 3rd pers sing pret subj): would be (from weorðan)

se – the, that

10 and his sweord ātēah, þæt hē hine ġeoffrode on þā ealdan wīsan.

11 Mid ðām ðe hē wolde þæt weorc beginnan, ðā clypode Godes engel arodlīċe of heofonum, "Abraham!" Hē andwyrde sōna.

12 Se engel him cwæð ðā tō: "Ne ācwele ðū þæt ċild, ne þīne hand ne āstreċe ofer his swēoran! Nū iċ oncnēow sōðlīċe þæt ðū swīðe ondrǣtst God, nū þū þīnne āncennedan sunu ofslēan woldest for him."

[handwritten annotations in margin: "together meon", "when"]

[handwritten translation:]

10 and his sword took up, in order to offer him in the old way. *that he might*

11. When he wanted the work begun, then called God's angel quickly from the Heavens, "abraham!" He answered right away.

12. The angel him said then to: "Do not (you) kill that child, nor stretch your hand *at all* further? over his neck! Now I recognize truly so you greatly fear God, now you your only son kill wanted for him

---

10 þæt hē hine ġeoffrode: "in order to offer him"
12 him cwæð ðā tō: "said then to him"
    ne ācwele ðū: "do not (you) kill"—imperatives frequently have an expressed subject in Old English, which can be omitted in translation
    ne þīne hand ne āstreċe: double negatives reinforce each other in Old English rather than cancelling each other out

ācwele (wk verb, imper sing): kill (from ācwellan)

āncennedan (adj, acc sing masc): only (begotten)

andwyrde (wk verb, 3rd pers sing pret indic): answered

arodlīċe (adv): quickly

āstreċe (wk verb, imper sing): stretch out (from āstreċċan)

ātēah (str verb, 3rd pers sing pres indic): took up; drew (from ātēon)

beginnan (str verb, infin): begin

ċild (str neut noun, acc sing): child

clypode (wk verb, 3rd pers sing pret indic): called; cried out (from clipian)

cwæð (str verb, 3rd pers sing pret indic): said (from cweðan)

ealdan (adj, acc sing fem): old

engel (str masc noun, nom sing): angel

God (str masc noun, acc sing): God

Godes (str masc noun, gen sing): God's

hand (str fem noun, acc sing): hand

heofonum (str masc noun, dat pl): the Heavens

hine (3rd pers pron, acc sing masc): him

iċ (1st pers pron, nom sing): I

mid ðām ðe (conj): when

ne (negative particle): not, nor

nū (adv): now

of (prep w. dat): from

ofer (prep w. acc): over

ġeoffrode (wk verb, 3rd pers sing pret subj): should offer, might offer

ofslēan (str verb, infin): kill

oncnēow (str verb, 1st pers sing pret indic): have recognized; have acknowledged (from oncnāwan)

ondrǣtst (str verb, 2nd pers sing pres indic): fear (from ondrǣdan)

se (dem pron, nom sing masc): the

sōðlīċe (adv): truly

sōna (adv): right away

sunu (masc noun, acc sing): son

swēoran (wk masc noun, acc sing): neck

sweord (str neut noun, acc sing): sword

swīðe (adv): greatly, very much

ðā (adv): then

þā (dem pron, acc sing fem): the

þæt (conj): that, so that

þæt (dem pron, acc sing neut): the, that

þīne (poss adj, acc sing fem): your

þīnne (poss adj, acc sing masc): your

ðū, þū (2nd pers pron, nom sing): you

weorc (str neut noun, acc sing): work

wīsan (wk fem noun, acc sing): way, manner

wolde (wk verb, 3rd pers sing pret indic): wanted (from willan)

woldest (wk verb, 2nd pers sing pret indic): wanted (from willan)

13 Þā beseah Abraham sōna underbæc and ġeseah ðǣr ānne ramm betweox þām brēmelum be ðām hornum ġehæft, and hē āhefde ðone ramm tō þǣre offrunge and hine þǣr ofsnāð Gode tō lāce for his sunu Isaac.

14 Hē hēt þā þā stōwe *Dominus uidit*, þæt is "God ġesiehð," and ġiet is ġesæġd swā, *In monte Dominus uidit*, þæt is "God ġesiehð on dūne."

15 Eft clypode se engel Abraham and cwæð,

13. Then looked Abraham immediately behind him and saw there one ram between the brambles/briars by the horns captured, and he lifted up one ram as the offering and him there killed as a sacrifice to God for his son Isaac

14. He called then the place the Lord sees, that is God sees, and yet is said so, on the mountain the Lord sees, that is "God sees on mountain."

15. Again called the angel Abraham and said,

---

13 **tō þǣre offrunge**: "as the offering"
 Gode tō lāce: "as a sacrifice to God"

āhefde (wk verb, 3rd pers sing pret indic): lifted up (from āhebban)

ānne (adj, acc sing masc): a, one

be (prep w. dat): by

beseah (str verb, 3rd pers sing pret indic): looked (from besēon)

betweox (prep w. dat): between, among

brēmelum (str masc noun, dat pl): brambles, briars

clypode (wk verb, 3rd pers sing pret indic): called (from clipian)

cwæð (str verb, 3rd pers sing pret indic): said (from cweðan)

Dominus uidit: "the Lord sees" (Latin)

dūne (str fem noun, dat sing): mountain

eft (adv): again

engel (str masc noun, nom sing): angel

ġiet (adv): yet, still

Gode (str masc noun, dat sing): to God

ġehæft (past part adj): captured, caught

hēt (str verb, 3rd pers sing pret indic): called, named (from hāten)

hine (3rd pers pron, acc sing masc): him, it

hornum (str masc noun, dat pl): horns

in monte: "on the mountain" (Latin)

lāce (str neut noun, dat sing): sacrifice; offering

offrunge (str fem noun, dat sing): offering

ofsnāð (str verb, 3rd pers sing pret indic): killed (by cutting) (from ofsnīðan)

ramm (str masc noun, acc sing): ram (male sheep)

ġesæġd (wk verb, past part): said (from secgan)

se (dem pron, nom sing masc): the

ġeseah (str verb, 3rd pers sing pret indic): saw (from sēon)

ġesiehð (str verb, 3rd pers sing pres indic): sees

sōna (adv): immediately

stōwe (str fem noun, acc sing): place

sunu (masc noun, acc sing): son

swā (adv): so, thus

þā (adv): then

þā (dem pron, acc sing fem): the, that

ðǣr, þǣr (adv): there

þǣre (dem pron, dat sing fem): the

þæt (dem pron, nom sing neut): that

þām, ðām (dem pron, dat pl): the

ðone (demons pron, acc sing masc): the

underbæc (adv): behind him

would not
ne + wolde

16 "Iċ swerie ðurh mē selfne, sǣġde se Ælmihtiga, nū ðū noldest ārian þīnum
āncennedan suna, ac ðē wæs mīn eġe māre þonne his līf,

17 iċ ðē nū bletsie and ðīnne ofspring ġemaniġfealde swā swā steorran on
heofonum and swā swā sandċeosol on sǣ. Þīn ofspring sceal āgan hira fēonda
gatu,

possessive

(myself)

16. I swear through me self, said the
almighty, now you (thou) *would not spare* did not want
to save your only begotten son, but to
you was (is/were) my fear * more than *greater* than
fear of me

his life

17. I you now bless and your descendants
(offspring) increase just as stars on
the sky and like sand on sea. Your
descendants shall own their enemies'
gates

---

16 **ðurh mē selfne:** God must swear on himself since there is nothing higher for him to invoke
    mīn eġe: "fear of me"

17 **āgan hira fēonda gatu:** i.e., dominate the cities of their enemies

ac (conj): but
Ælmihtiga (prop name, nom sing): Almighty
āgan (wk verb infin): own, possess
āncennedan (adj, dat sing masc): only begotten
ārian (wk verb infin w. dat): honour, save, spare
bletsie (wk verb, 1st pers sing pres indic): bless (from bletsian)
eġe (str masc noun, nom sing): awe, dread, fear
fēonda (str masc noun, gen pl): enemies'
gatu (str neut noun, acc pl): gates
heofonum (str masc noun, dat pl): the Heavens, the sky
hira (3rd pers pron, gen pl): their
iċ (1st pers pron, nom sing): I
līf (str neut noun, nom sing): life
ġemaniġfealde (wk verb, 1st pers sing): multiply; increase (from ġemaniġfealdan)
māre (adj, nom sing masc): greater, more
mē (1st pers pron, acc sing): me
mīn (1st pers pron, gen sing): my
noldest (wk verb, 3rd pers sing pret indic): did not want to, would not (from willan)
nū (adv): now
ofspring (str masc noun, nom/acc sing): descendants, offspring
sǣ (str masc noun, dat sing): sea
sǣġde (wk verb, 3rd pers sing pret indic): said (from secgan)
sandċeosol (str masc noun, nom sing): sand
sceal (wk verb, 3rd pers sing pres indic): shall (from sculan)
selfne (pron, acc sing masc): self
steorran (wk masc noun, nom pl): stars
suna (masc noun, dat sing): son
swā swā (conj): like, just as
swerie (str verb, 1st pers sing pres indic): swear, vow (from swerian)
ðē (2nd pers pron, acc sing): you
ðē (2nd pers pron, dat sing): to you
þīn (2nd pers pron, gen sing): your
ðīnne (poss adj, acc sing masc): your
þīnum (poss adj, dat sing masc): your
þonne (conj): than
ðū (2nd pers pron, nom sing): you
ðurh (prep w. acc): through, by means of
wæs (anom verb, 3rd pers sing pret indic): was (from bēon)

18 and on þinum sæde bēoð ealle ðēoda ġebletsodę <u>for þām ðe</u> þū *because* ġehīersumodest mīnre hǣse ðus."

19 Abraham ðā ġecierde sōna tō his cnapum and fērdon him hām swā mid heofonlīċre bletsunge.

18. and on your seed will be all blessed because you obeyed my command in this way.

19. Abraham then returned immediately to his servants and they traveled home so with heavenly blessing

---

18 **mīnre hǣse: hīersumian** takes the dative case for its object
19 **fērdon him hām: him** is reflexive and does not need to be translated

bēoð (anom verb, 3rd pers pl pres indic): will be (from bēon)

ġebletsode (wk verb, past part nom pl fem): blessed (from bletsian)

bletsunge (str fem noun, dat sing): blessing

ġeċierde (wk verb, 3rd pers sing pret indic): returned (from cierran)

cnapum (wk masc noun, dat pl): servants

ealle (adj, nom pl fem): all

fērdon (wk verb, pl pret indic): (they) travelled (from fēran)

for þām ðe (conj): because

hǣse (str fem noun, dat sing): command

hām (adv): home, homewards

heofonlīċre (adj, dat sing fem): heavenly

ġehīersumodest (wk verb, 2nd pers sing pret indic): obeyed (from (ġe)hīersumian)

mid (prep w. dat): with

mīnre (poss adj, dat sing fem): my

sǣde (str neut noun, dat sing): seed, offspring, descendants

sōna (adv): immediately

swā (adv): thus, so, in this way

ðā (adv): then

ðēoda (str fem noun, nom pl): peoples, nations

þīnum (poss adj, dat sing neut): your

þū (2nd pers pron, nom sing): you

ðus (adv): thus, in this way

The Birth of Jesus (Luke 2:1–21)

1 Sōþliċe on þām dagum wæs ġeworden ġebod fram þām Cāsere Augusto þæt
eall ymbehwyrft wære tōmearcod.

2 Þēos tōmearcodnes wæs ǣryst ġeworden fram þām dēman Sȳriġe Cīrino

3 and ealle hīġ ēodon and syndrie fērdon on hyra ċeastre.

4 Ðā fērde Iosep fram Galilea of þǣre ċeastre Nazareth on Iūdēisce ċeastre
Dauides sēo is ġenemned Bethleem forþam þe hē wæs of Dauides hūse and
hīrede.

5 He fērde mid Marian þe him beweddod wæs and wæs ġeeacnod.

6 Sōðlice wæs ġeworden, þā hī þǣr wǣron, hire dagas wǣron ġefyllede þæt hēo
cende,

[handwritten notes:]

1. Truly on the days happened command from the Caesar Augustus that all the circumference (of the Earth) should be described

2. [These censes first happened from the judge] These/Those census were first carried out by the governor of Syria Cirinus

3. and all he see and separately go on his emperor

4. They travel to Iosep from Galilea of

---

1 **ymbehwyrft**: literally this word refers to the surface of a disc—the world was considered to
be round and flat in the early Middle Ages

2 **fram þām dēman Sȳriġe Cīrino**: (was first carried out) "by the governor of Syria Cirinus"

ǣryst *adv*: first
and *conj*: and
Augustus *prop name*: Augustus Caesar (**Augusto** *dat sing*)
beweddod *past part adj*: married
ġebod *neut noun*: command
cāsere *masc noun*: emperor (**cāsere** *dat sing*)
ċeaster *fem noun*: city (**ċeastre** *acc/dat sing*)
cennan *wk verb*: give birth (**cende** *3rd pers sing pret indic*)
Cīrinus *prop name*: Cirinus (**Cīrino** *(Latin) dat sing*)
dæġ *masc noun*: day (**dagas** *nom pl*; **dagum** *dat pl*)
Dauid *prop name*: David (**Dauides** *gen sing*)
dēma *masc noun*: judge, governor (**dēman** *dat sing*)
ġeeacnod *past part adj*: pregnant
eall *adj*: all (**ealle** *nom/acc pl*)
ēodon: see **gān**
fēran *wk verb*: go, travel (**fērde** *3rd pers sing pret indic*; **fērdon** *pl pret indic*)
forþām, forþām þe *conj*: because
fram *prep*: from, by
fyllan *wk verb*: fill, fulfill, complete (**ġefyllede** *past part nom pl masc*)
gān *anom verb*: go (**ēodon** *pl pret indic*)
hē, hēo, hit *pers pron*: he, she, it (**hīġ, hī** *nom/acc pl*; **him** *dat sing masc; dat pl*; **hire, hyre** *dat/gen sing fem*; **hyra, heora** *gen pl*)
hīred *masc noun*: household, family (**hīrede** *dat sing*)
hūs *neut noun*: house, family (**hūse** *dat sing*)
Iosep *prop name*: Joseph
Iūdēisc *adj*: in or of Judaea (**Iūdēisce** acc sing fem)
Maria *prop name*: Mary (**Marian** *dat sing*)
mid *prep*: with
nemnan *wk verb*: name (**ġenemned** *past part*)
of *prep*: from, out of
on *prep*: on, in; onto, into
sōþliċe *adv*: truly, indeed
syndrie *adv*: separately, individually
Sȳria *prop name*: Syria (**Sȳriġe** *(Latin) gen sing*)
ðā, þā *adv and conj*: then, when
þǣr *adv*: there
þæt *conj*: that
þe, ðe *rel pron*: who, which, that
þes *dem*: this, (in pl) these (**þēos** *nom sing fem*)
tōmearcian *wk verb*: describe, note down (**tōmearcod** *past part*)
tōmearcodnes *fem noun*: census
wǣre tōmearcod: should be described (i.e., inventoried)
wæs ġeworden: happened, came to pass
ymbehwyrft *masc noun*: the circumference (of the world)

7 and hēo cende hyre frumcennedan sunu and hine mid ċildclāþum bewand and hine on binne ālēde, forþām þe hīġ næfdon rūm on cumena hūse.

8 And hyrdas wǣron on þām ylcan rīċe waciende and nihtwæċċan healdende ofer heora heorda.

9 Þā stōd Drihtnes engel wiþ hīġ and Godes beorhtnes him ymbesceān and hī him myċelum ēġe ādrēdon.

10 And se engel him tō cwæð, "Nelle ġē ēow ādrǣdan. Sōþliċe nū iċ ēow bodie myċelne ġefēan se bið eallum folce

11 forþām tōdæġ ēow ys hǣlend ācenned se is Drihten Crīst on Dauides ċeastre.

---

7 **mid ċildclāþum**: "with baby-cloths"—the King James version calls these "swaddling-clothes"
9 **hī him ... ādrēdon**: "they were afraid"—**him** is reflexive, so omit it in translation
10 **Nelle ġē ēow ādrǣdan**: "do not be afraid"—**ēow** is likewise reflexive

ācennan *wk verb*: give birth to (ācenned *past part*)

ādrǣdan *Class 7 weak verb*: dread, fear (ādrēdon *pl pret indic*)

ālecgan *wk verb*: lay, put down (ālēde *3rd pers sing pret indic*)

bēon *anom verb*: to be (biŏ *3rd pers sing pres indic*; wæs *3rd pers sing pret indic*; wǣre *3rd pers sing pret subj* ("should be"); wǣron *pl pret indic*; ys, is *3rd pers sing pres indic*)

beorhtnes *fem noun*: brightness

bewindan *Class 3 str verb*: wrap (bewand *3rd pers sing pret indic*)

binn *fem noun*: bin, basket, manger (binne *acc sing*)

bodian *wk verb*: proclaim (bodie *1st pers sing pres indic*)

ċildclaþas *masc pl noun*: baby clothes (ċildclaþum baby blankets)

Crīst *prop name*: Christ

cumena hūs *neut noun*: guest house, inn

cweŏan *Class 5 str verb*: say (cwæŏ *3rd pers sing pret indic*)

Drihten *masc noun*: the Lord (Drihtnes *gen sing*)

eall *adj*: all (eallum *dat sing neut*)

ēġe *masc noun*: awe, dread (ēġe *dat sing*)

engel *masc noun*: angel

ġefēa *masc noun*: joy (ġefēan *acc sing*)

folc *neut noun*: people, nation (folce *dat sing*)

frumcenned *past part adj*: first-born (frumcennedan *acc sing masc*)

ġē *pron*: you (pl.) (ēow *dat*)

God *masc noun*: God (Godes *gen sing*)

habban *anom verb*: to have (næfdon *pl pret indic negative*: did not have)

hǣlend *masc noun*: saviour

hē, hēo, hit *pers pron*: he, she, it (hine *acc sing masc*)

healdan *Class 7 str verb*: hold, keep, maintain (healdende *pres part*)

heord *fem noun*: herd, flock (heorda *acc pl*)

hyrde *masc noun*: shepherd (hyrdas *nom pl*)

iċ *pers pron*: I

myċel *adj*: great, much (myċelum *dat sing masc*; myċelne *acc sing masc*)

næfdon: see habban

nelle: see willan

nihtwǣċċe *fem noun*: night watch (nihtwǣċċan *acc sing*)

nū *adv*: now

ofer *prep*: over

rīċe *neut noun*: kingdom (rīċe *dat sing*)

rūm *masc noun*: room, space

standan *Class 6 str verb*: stand (stōd *3rd pers sing pret indic*)

sunu *masc noun*: son

tō *prep*: to

tōdæġ *adv*: today

wacian *wk verb*: be awake (waciende *pres part*)

willan *anom verb*: to wish, desire (nelle *imper pl*: do not)

wiþ *prep*: with, by, near

ylca *adj*: same (ylcan *dat sing neut*)

ymbescīnan *Class 1 str verb*: shine around (ymbesceān *3rd per sing pret indic*)

12 And þis tācen ēow byð: Ġē ġemētað ān ċild hreġlum bewunden and on binne ālēd."

13 And þā wæs fǣringa ġeworden mid þām engle myċelnes heofonliċes werodes God heriendra and þus cweþendra:

14 "Gode sȳ wuldor on hēahnesse and on eorðan sybb mannum gōdes willan."

15 And hit wæs ġeworden þā ðā englas tō heofene fērdon, þā hyrdas him betwynan sprǣcon and cwǣdon, "Uton faran tō Bethlēem and ġesēon þæt word þe ġeworden is þæt Drihten ūs ætȳwde."

---

12 **tācen ēow byð**: "will be a sign to you"—there is no separate future tense in Old English

13 **myċelnes heofonliċes werodes God heriendra and þus cweþendra**: "a multitude of heavenly host praising God and saying thus"—notice that the present participle adjectives after the noun are plural, responding to the idea that there are many angels, even though the noun **werod** is singular

14 **Gode sȳ wuldor**: "(May there be) glory to God"

15 **þæt word þe ġeworden is**: "the news that has taken place" or "the prophecy that has become real"; also, of course, a reference to John 1:14, "And the Word was made flesh, and dwelt among us"

ætȳwan *wk verb*: reveal, make known (**ætȳwde** *3rd pers sing pret indic*)

ān *numer*: one, a

ālecgan *wk verb*: lay, put down (**ālēd** *past part*)

beon *anom verb*: to be (**biŏ, bȳŏ** *3rd pers sing pres indic*; **sȳ** *3rd pers sing pres subj*)

betwynan *prep*: between, among

bewindan *Class 3 str verb*: wrap (**bewunden** *past part*)

ċild *neut noun*: baby, child (**ċilde** *dat sing*)

cweŏan *Class 5 str verb*: say (**cwǣdon** *pl pret indic*; **cweþendra** *pres part gen pl*)

engel *masc noun*: angel (**englas** *nom pl*; **engle** *dat sing*)

eorŏe *fem noun*: earth (**eorŏan** *dat sing*)

fǣringa *adv*: suddenly

faran *Class 6 str verb*: go, travel

gōd *adj*: good (**gōdes** *gen sing masc*)

God *masc noun*: God (**Gode** *dat sing*)

hēahnes *fem noun*: height, highness (**hēahnesse** *dat sing*)

heofon *masc noun*: heaven (**heofene** *dat sing*)

heofonliċ *adj*: heavenly (**heofonliċes** *gen sing neut*)

herian *wk verb*: praise (**heriendra** *pres part gen pl*)

hreġl *neut noun*: clothing, garment (**hreġlum** *dat pl*)

mann *masc noun*: man (**mannum** *dat pl*)

ġemētan *wk verb*: meet (**ġemētaŏ** *pl pres indic*)

myċelnes *fem noun*: multitude

on hēahnesse: (translating Latin *in excelsis*) in the highest

ġesēon *Class 5 str verb*: see

sprēcan *Class 5 str verb*: speak (**sprǣcon** *pl pret indic*)

sybb *fem noun*: peace, friendship

tācen *neut noun*: sign

þes *dem*: this, (in *pl*) these (**þis** *nom sing neut*)

þus *adv*: thus, in this way

uton *idiomatic verb*: let us

werod *neut noun*: army, host (**werodes** *gen sing*)

willa *masc noun*: will, purpose, intent (**willan** *gen sing*)

word *neut noun*: word utterance, report, story

ġeworden is: has happened

wuldor *neut noun*: glory

16 And hīġ efstende cōmon and ġemetton Marrian and Iosep and þæt ċild on binne ālēd.

17 Þā hī þæt ġesāwon, þā oncnēowon hīġ be þām worde þe him gesǣd wæs be þām ċilde.

18 And ealle þā ðe ġehyrdon wundredon be þām þe him þā hyrdas sǣdon.

19 Maria ġehēold ealle þās word on hyre heortan smēagende.

20 Ðā ġewendon hām þā hyrdas God wuldriende and heriende on eallum þām ðe hī ġehyrdon and ġesāwon, swā tō him ġecweden wæs.

21 Æfter þām þe eahta dagas ġefyllede wǣron þæt ðæt ċild emsnyden wǣre, his nama wæs Hǣlend se wæs fram engle ġenemned ǣr hē on innoðe ġeeacnod wǣre.

17 **oncnēowon ... be**: "knew [him] ... by"
18 **wundredon be þām**: "marvelled about that"
20 **on eallum þām**: "in all those things"
21 **Hǣlend se wæs fram engle ġenemned**: the name Jesus (literally, "God saves") was given to Joseph in a dream, according to Matthew 1:21

ǣr *conj*: before
æfter þām þe *conj*: after
be *prep*: by, according to, about
cuman *Class 4 str verb*: come (cōmon *pl pret indic*)
cweðan *Class 5 str verb*: say (ġecweden *past part*)
eahta *numeral*: eight
efstan *wk verb*: hurry (efstende *pres part*)
emsnīdan *Class 1 str verb*: circumcise (emsnyden *past part*)
fyllan *wk verb*: fill, fulfill, complete (ġefyllede *past part nom pl masc*)
ġeeacnod *past part adj* (of a fetus): conceived
herian *wk verb*: praise (heriende *pres part*)
ġehyran *wk verb*: hear (ġehyrdon *pl pret indic*)
ġewendan *wk verb*: to (ġewendon *pl pret indic*)
Hǣlend: Saviour
hām *adv*: home
hē, hēo, hit *pers pron*: he, she, it (hīġ, hī *nom/acc pl*; him *dat pl*; hyre */gen sing fem*)
healdan *Class 7 str verb*: hold, keep, maintain (ġehēold *3rd pers sing pret indic*)
heorte *fem noun*: heart (heortan *dat sing*)
innoð *masc noun*: womb, entrails, stomach (innoðe *dat sing*)
Maria *prop name*: Mary (Marrian *acc sing*)
ġemētan *wk verb*: meet (ġemetton *pl pret indic*)
nama *masc noun*: name
nemnan *wk verb*: name (ġenemned *past part*)
oncnāwan *Class 7 str verb*: understand, know, recognize (oncnēowon *pl pret indic*)
secgan *wk verb*: say (gesǣd *past part*; sǣdon *pl pret indic*)
ġesēon *Class 5 str verb*: see (ġesāwon *pl pret indic*)
smēagan *wk verb*: consider, ponder, reflect (smēagende *pres part*)
swā *adv and conj*: as
word *neut noun*: word, utterance, report, story (word *acc pl*; worde *dat sing*)
wuldrian *wk verb*: praise, glorify (wuldriende *pres part*)
wundrian *wk verb*: marvel, wonder (wundredon *pl pret indic*)

The Story of Ohthere

Introduction

The story of Ohthere is an insertion into a translation (from Latin) of a history of the world by Paulus Orosius. Orosius was a fifth-century Spanish cleric (flourished ca. 415) who wrote his *Historia adversus paganos* ("History Against the Pagans"), a history of the world, to refute pagan claims that the coming of Christianity was responsible for recent disasters in Europe, especially the Germanic invasions. Possibly the Old English Orosius was one of the works of translation commissioned by King Alfred the Great (who reigned from 871 to 899 as King of Wessex) as part of his educational program proclaimed in the preface to Gregory the Great's *Pastoral Care*. The story of Ohthere's voyage is added to the first section of Orosius' history, which gives a brief geography of the world as known to early medieval Europeans. Another narrative (the voyage of Wulfstan) and a fairly complex account of the locations of continental Germanic peoples were also added there. It seems a fair presumption that the intent of these additions was to complete and extend Orosius' account where it was seen to be lacking: in the description of the northern part of Western Europe. (In this context it is noteworthy that no description of the island of Britain is given—it is the geography of far-away places that the translators wanted to record.)

Other than his name, where he came from, and the one voyage described here, we don't know much at all about Ohthere himself. Ohthere was a "Norþmann," or Norwegian, and although we do not know the circumstances of his meeting with Alfred, we can situate the meeting within a century of violent contact between Norse-speaking people like Ohthere and the Anglo-Saxons. Alfred himself ruled during the most brutal period of the first wave of Viking attack on Britain and stemmed the tide of invasion, confining the Vikings to a large area of the eastern half of England, the Danelaw, over which they then ruled while Alfred and his successors ruled the remaining part. It seems clear that Ohthere himself was not (at least primarily) one of the Viking attackers, but a merchant or trader who encountered the Anglo-Saxon king under peaceful circumstances. To support this presumption, we have the indication that Alfred was presented with trade goods (walrus ivory) and we have the rather lengthy and detailed narrative itself, with sailing times, names of peoples, and descriptions of territories.

The Voyage of Ohthere

1 Ohthere sǣde his hlāforde, Ælfrede cyninge,[1] þæt hē ealra Norðmonna norþmest būde.

2 Hē cwæð þæt hē būde on þǣm lande norþweardum wiþ þā Westsǣ.[2]

3 Hē sǣde þēah þæt þæt land sīe swīþe lang norþ þonan, ac hit is eal wēste, būton on fēawum stōwum styċċemǣlum wīciaþ Finnas,[3] on huntoðe on wintra, and on sumera on fiscaþe be þǣre sǣ.

4 Hē sǣde þæt hē æt sumum ċirre wolde fandian hū longe þæt land norþryhte lǣġe, oþþe hwæðer ǣnig mon be norðan þǣm wēstenne būde.

5 Þā fōr hē norþryhte[4] be þǣm lande.

6 Lēt him ealne wēġ þæt wēste land on ðæt stēorbord, and þā wīdsǣ on ðæt bæcbord þrīe dagas.

7 Þā wæs hē swā feor norþ swā þā hwælhuntan firrest faraþ.

8 Þā fōr hē þā ġīet norþryhte swā feor swā hē meahte on þǣm ōþrum þrīm dagum ġesiġlan.

9 Þā bēag þæt land þǣr ēastryhte, oþþe sēo sǣ in on ðæt lond, hē nysse hwæðer, būton hē wisse ðæt hē ðǣr bād westan windes and hwōn norþan, and siġlde þā ēast be lande swā swā hē meahte on fēower dagum ġesiġlan.

10 Þā sceolde hē ðǣr bīdan ryhtnorþanwindes, forðǣm þæt land bēag þǣr sūþryhte, oþþe sēo sǣ in on ðæt land, hē nysse hwæþer.

11 Þā siġlde hē þonan sūðryhte be lande swā swā hē mehte on fīf dagum ġesiġlan.

12 Ðā læġ þǣr ān miċel ēa up in on þæt land.

13 Þā ċirdon hīe up in on ðā ēa, forþǣm hīe ne dorston forþ bi þǣre ēa siġlan for unfriþe, forþǣm þæt land wæs eall ġebūn on ōþre healfe þǣre ēas.

14 Ne mette hē ǣr nān ġebūn land, siþþan hē from his āgnum hām fōr, ac him wæs ealne wēġ wēste land on þæt stēorbord, būtan fiscerum and fugelerum and huntum, and þæt wǣron eall Finnas, and him wæs ā wīdsǣ on ðæt bæcbord.

---

1 **his hlāforde, Ælfrede cyninge:** It seems most unlikely that Alfred was really Ohthere's lord; more likely this expression either indicates a ceremony of obeisance required of merchants or simply reflects the real-world conversation opening, "My lord, King Alfred.... "

2 **on þǣm lande ... Westsǣ:** "in the northward (part of the) land by the North Atlantic."

3 **Finnas:** Sámi people, the aboriginal inhabitants of the northern parts of Norway, Sweden, and Finland and of the Kola Peninsula in Russia. They were nomadic hunters and fishers at this period, and the Ohthere story describes them as camping (using the verb **wīcian**) as opposed to the Biarmians and Norwegians who settle the land (the Ohthere story uses **būan**).

4 **norþryhte:** "directly north," but, as becomes apparent, following the coast of Norway closely, so in fact in a northeasterly direction.

15 Þā Beormas[5] hæfdon swīþe wel ġebūn hira land, ac hīe ne dorston þǣron cuman.

16 Ac þāra Terfinna land wæs eal wēste, būton ðǣr huntan ġewīcodon, oþþe fisceras, oþþe fugeleras.

17 Fela spella him sǣdon þā Beormas ǣgþer ġe of hiera āgnum lande ġe of þǣm landum þe ymb hīe ūtan wǣron, ac hē nyste hwæt þæs sōþes wæs,[6] forþǣm hē hit self ne ġeseah.

18 Þā Finnas, him þūhte, and þā Beormas sprǣcon nēah ān ġeþēode.

19 Swīþost hē fōr ðider, tōēacan þæs landes scēawunge, for þǣm horshwælum, forðǣm hīe habbað swīþe æþele bān on hiora tōþum.[7]

20 Þā tēð hīe brohton sume[8] þǣm cyninge, and hiora hȳd bið swīðe gōd tō sciprāpum.

21 Se hwæl bið micle lǣssa þonne ōðre hwalas: ne bið hē lengra ðonne syfan elna lang.[9]

22 Ac on his āgnum lande is se betsta hwælhuntað: þā[10] bēoð eahta and fēowertiġes elna lange, and þā mǣstan fiftiġes elna lange.

23 Þāra hē sǣde þæt hē syxa sum ofslōge syxtiġ on twām dagum.

24 Hē wæs swȳðe spēdiġ man on þǣm æhtum þe heora spēda on bēoð,[11] þæt is, on wildrum.

25 Hē hæfde þā ġȳt, ðā hē þone cyningc sōhte, tamra dēora unbebohtra syx hund.

26 Þā dēor hī hātað "hrānas."

27 Þāra wǣron syx stælhrānas.

28 Ðā bēoð swȳðe dȳre mid Finnum, forðǣm hȳ fōð þā wildan hrānas mid.

29 Hē wæs mid þǣm fyrstum mannum on þǣm lande; næfde hē þēah mā ðonne twentiġ hrȳðera and twentiġ scēapa and twentiġ swȳna, and þæt lytle þæt hē erede hē erede mid horsan.

---

5 **Beormas**: Biarmians, a people of what is now part of northwest Russia, about whom we know very little for sure and for whose existence and location at this time the Ohthere story is the main source. Their land, Bjarmaland, is mentioned in the Norse sagas as lying near the River Dvina, which does not match the Ohthere sailing directions. Possibly they were Karelians, whose language, like that of the Sámi people, is Finno-Ugric and related to Finnish.

6 **hwæt þæs sōþes wæs**: literally, "what was of the truth," i.e., what parts of what they told him were true.

7 **æþele bān on hiora tōþum**: Walrus ivory comes from the tusk of the walrus, a modified canine tooth.

8 **Þā tēð hīe brohton sume**: "they brought some of the teeth."

9 **syfan elna lang**: the male Atlantic walrus ranges up to about 3 metres in length.

10 **þā**: not walruses, in this sentence, but true whales.

11 **on þǣm æhtum ... on bēoð**: "in the goods of which their wealth consists."

30 Ac hyra ār is mǣst on þǣm gafole þe ðā Finnas him ġyldað.

31 Þæt gafol bið on dēora fellum and on fugela feðerum and hwales bāne and on þǣm sciprāpum þe bēoð of hwæles hȳde ġeworht and of sēoles.

32 Ǣġhwilċ ġylt be hys ġebyrdum.

33 Se byrdesta sceall ġyldan fiftȳne mearðes fell and fīf hrānes and ān beran fel and tȳn ambra feðra and berenne kyrtel oððe yterenne and twēġen sciprāpas, ǣġþer sȳ[12] syxtiġ elna lang, ōþer sȳ of hwæles hȳde ġeworht, ōþer of sīoles.

34 Hē sǣde ðæt Norðmanna land wǣre swȳþe lang and swȳðe smæl.

35 Eal þæt his man āþer oððe ettan oððe erian mæġ,[13] þæt lið wið ðā sǣ and þæt is þēah on sumum stōwum swȳðe clūdiġ, and licgað wilde mōras wið ēastan and wið uppon,[14] emnlange þǣm bȳnum lande.

36 On þǣm mōrum eardiað Finnas, and þæt bȳne land is ēasteweard brādost and symle swā norðor swā smǣlre.[15]

37 Ēastewerd hit mæġ bīon syxtiġ mīla brād oþþe hwene brǣdre, and middeweard þrītiġ oððe brādre, and norðeweard, hē cwæð, þǣr hit smālost wǣre, þæt hit mihte bēon þrēora mīla brād tō þǣm mōre, and se mōr syðþan, on sumum stōwum swā brād swā man mæġ on twām wucum oferfēran, and on sumum stōwum swā brād swā man mæġ on syx dagum oferfēran.

38 Þonne is tōemnes þǣm lande sūðeweardum, on ōðre healfe þæs mōres, Swēoland, oþ þæt land norðeweard, and tōemnes þǣm lande norðeweardum Cwēna land.

39 Þā Cwēnas[16] herġiað hwīlum on ðā Norðmen ofer ðone mōr, hwīlum þā Norðmen on hȳ.

40 And þǣr sint swīðe micle meras fersce ġeond þā mōras, and berað þā Cwēnas hyra scypu ofer land on ðā meras and þanon herġiað on ðā Norðmen; hȳ habbað swȳðe lytle scypa and swȳðe lēohte.

41 Ohthere sǣde þæt sīo scīr hātte Halgoland þe hē on būde.

42 Hē cwæð þæt nān man ne būde be norðan him.

43 Þonne is ān port on sūðeweardum þǣm lande, þone man hǣt Scīringeshēal.

---

12 **ǣġþer sȳ**: "each to be."

13 **Eal þæt his man ... mæġ**: "all of it that one can either use for grazing or plow for crops."

14 **wið uppon**: "above," i.e., further inland.

15 **ēasteweard ... smǣlre**: Probably a simple error, since given actual Norwegian geography (the peninsula extending from southwest to northeast) the opposition should really be between western and northern, but just possibly an artifact of a confusingly abbreviated description of the actual situation: most of the arable land and the pasture in Norway is on the eastern side of the southern tip of the peninsula around Oslo; the remaining pockets are on the western coast and become fewer and smaller the further north you travel.

16 **Þā Cwēnas**: likely a Sámi people.

44 Þyder hē cwæð þæt man ne mihte ġeseġlian on ānum monðe, ġyf man on niht wīcode, and ælce dæġe hæfde ambyrne wind, and ealle ðā hwīle hē sceal seġlian be lande, and on þæt stēorbord him bið ærest Īraland, and þonne ðā īġland þe synd betux Īralande and þissum lande.[17]

45 Þonne is þis land oð hē cymð tō Scīrincgeshēale, and ealne wēġ on þæt bæcbord Norðwēġ.

46 Wið sūðan þone Scīringeshēal fylð swȳðe myċel sæ[18] up in on ðæt lond, sēo is brādre þonne ǣniġ man ofer sēon mæġe, and is Gotland on ōðre healfe onġēan and siððan Sillende.

47 Sēo sæ līð mæniġ hund mīla up in on þæt land.

48 And of Scīringeshēale hē cwæð þæt hē seġlode on fīf dagan tō þǣm porte þe mon hǣt æt Hǣþum, se stent betuh Wīnedum and Seaxum and Angle, and hȳrð in on Dene.

49 Ðā hē þiderweard seġlode fram Scīringeshēale, þā wæs him on þæt bæcbord Denamearc, and on þæt stēorbord wīdsæ þrȳ dagas; and þā, twēġen dagas ǣr hē tō Hǣþum cōme, him wæs on þæt stēorbord Gotland and Sillende and īġlanda fela.

50 On þǣm landum eardodon Engle, ǣr hī hider on land cōman.

51 And hym wæs ðā twēġen dagas on ðæt bæcbord þā īġland þe in Denemearce hȳrað.

---

17 These sailing directions are unlikely from several points of view: the sailing time of more than a month is impossibly long, and the mention of Ireland as on the starboard has caused scholars incalculable grief. Some of the problems are removed if instead of considering this sentence to describe the route from Halgoland to Sciringesheal, as has been the common assumption, it is taken as being a possible route from the west of England to Sciringesheal via the Atlantic side of Ireland, the Hebrides ("the islands that are between Ireland and this land"), and then the tip and eastern coast of Scotland, at which point Norway is ("all the way") on the port side. But this would then seem to be a very strange route, both dangerous because of exposure to Atlantic swells, and unnecessarily long—the whole description may be the result either of error or of deliberate disinformation.

18 **swȳðe myċel sæ**: i.e., the Baltic.

The Voyage of Ohthere: Glossary

Entries are in alphabetical order except that the ge- prefix is ignored for alphabetization. The letters thorn (Þ/þ) and eth (Ð/ð) are alphabetized following letter t; letter ash (Æ/æ) is alphabetized as if it were the sequence AE (ae). Headwords of entries for verbs are the infinitive form unless otherwise indicated; headwords for nouns are nominative singular unless otherwise indicated. Accusative singular forms of nouns are identical to the nominative singular form unless otherwise noted. All other inflected forms of nouns and pronouns appear in alphabetical order within the entry and are identified as to case and number.

Abbreviations used in this glossary:

acc = accusative	masc = masculine
adj = adjective	neut = neuter
adv = adverb	nom = nominative
anom = anomalous	past part = past participle
compar = comparative	pers = personal
conj = conjunction	pers = person
correl = correlative	pl = plural
dat = dative	poss = possessive
dem = demonstrative	prep = preposition
fem = feminine	pres = present tense
gen = genitive	pres part = present participle
imper = imperative	pret = preterite (past) tense
impers = impersonal	pron = pronoun
indef = indefinite	prop = proper
indic = indicative	rel = relative
infin = infinitive	sing = singular
inflect infin = inflected infinitive	str = strong
inst = instrumental	subj = subjunctive
interj = interjection	superl = superlative
interrog = interrogative	wk = weak

ā *adv*: forever, always (14)

ac *conj*: but, however, but on the contrary, and (3, 14, etc.)

ǣġhwilċ *pron nom sing*: each (one) (32)

ǣġþer *pron nom sing*: each (33)

        ǣġþer ġe ... ġe both ... and (17)

æht *fem noun*: possession, wealth

æhtum *dat pl* (24)

ǣlċe *adj inst sing masc*: each (40)

Ælfrede *prop name, dat sing*: Alfred (1)

ǣniġ *adj nom sing masc*: any (4, 46)

ǣr *adv and conj*: previously; before (14, 49, 50)

        ǣrest *adv*: first (44)

æt *prep with dat*: at, from (4, 48)

æt Hǣþum *see* Hǣþum

æþele *adj acc pl neut*: noble, excellent (19)

āgnum *adj dat sing masc/neut*: (14, 17, 22)

amber *neut noun*: measure of one amber (an unknown quantity, but a dry or
        liquid measure)

        ambra *acc pl* (33)

        ambyrne *adj acc sing neut*: favourable (44)

ān *adj*: a, an, one, only (12, 18, 33, 43)

        ānum *dat sing masc* (44)

and *conj*: and (3, etc.)

Angle *masc pl noun*: the Angles (48)

ānum: see ān

ār *fem noun*: honour, worth, property, revenue (30)

āþer oððe ... oððe *conj*: either ... or (35)

bād: see bīdan

bæcbord *neut noun*: left side of a ship, port side, larboard (6, 14, 45, 49, 51)

bān *neut noun*: bone

        bān *acc pl* (19)

        bāne *dat sing* (31)

be, bi *prep with dat*: by, alongside, to the (north, etc.), according to (3, etc.)

        be norðan *prep*: to the north of (4, 42)

bēag: see būgan

bēon, bīon *verb*: to be (37)

        bēoð *pl pres indic* (22, 28, 31)

        bið *3rd pers sing pres indic* (20, 21, 31, 44)

        is *3rd pers sing pres indic* (3, etc.)

sīe, sȳ *3rd pers sing pres subj*: (3, 33)
sint, synd *pl pres indic* (40, 44)
wǣre *3rd pers sing pret subj* (34, 37)
wǣron *pl pret indic* (14, 17, 27)
wæs *3rd pers sing pret indic* (7, etc.)
Beormas *prop name nom pl*: Biarmians, a people of what is now part of
    northwest Russia (15, 18)
beran *str verb*: to bear, carry
    beraδ *pl pres indic* (40)
bera *masc noun*: bear
    beran *gen sing* (33)
beren *adj*: made of bear skin
    berenne *acc sing masc* (33)
betsta *superl adj*: best (22)
betux, betuh *prep with dat*: between (44, 48)
bi: see **be**
bīdan *str verb with gen*: to wait (for) (10)
    bād *3rd pers sing pret indic* (9)
biδ: see **bēon**
brād *adj*: broad (37)
    brādost *superl*: broadest (36)
    brǣdre, brādre *compar*: broader (37, 46)
bringan *str verb*: to bring
    brohton *pl pret indic* (20)
būan *wk verb*: to stay, dwell, live
    būde *3rd pers sing pret indic* (1, 2, 4, 41, 42)
    ġebūn *past part*: settled, inhabited (13, 14, 15)
    bȳne *past part* (36)
    bȳnum *past part dat sing* (35)
būgan *str verb*: to bow down, turn, bend, stoop
    bēag *3rd pers sing pret indic*: turned (9, 10)
būde, ġebūn: see **būan**
būton *prep with dat and conj*: without, except, but, only; except that (3, 9,
    14, 16)
bȳne, bȳnum: see **būan**
byrdesta *adj*: highest born, highest ranked (33)
ġebyrd *fem noun*: birth, rank, condition
    ġebyrdum *dat pl* (32)

ċirr *masc noun*: turn, change, time, occasion

    ċirre *dat sing* (4)

ċirran *wk verb*: to turn, cause to move

    ċirdon *3rd pers sing pret indic*: turned (13)

clūdiġ *adj*: rocky (35)

cuman *str verb*: to come, approach, get to, attain (15)

    cōman *pl pret indic* (50)

    cōme *3rd pers sing pret indic* (49)

    cymð *3rd pers sing pres indic* (45)

Cwēnas *masc noun pl*: a Sámi people (39, 40)

    Cwēna *gen pl* (38)

cweþan *str verb*: to say

    cwæð *3rd pers sing pret indic* (2, 37, 42, 44, 48)

cymð: see **cuman**

cyning *masc noun*: king

    cyningc *acc sing* (25)

    cyninge *dat sing* (1, 20)

dæġ *masc noun*: day

    dæġe *dat sing* (44)

    dagan *dat pl* (48)

    dagas *nom/acc pl* (6, 49, 51)

    dagum *dat pl* (8, 9, 11, 23, 37)

Denamearc *fem noun*: Denmark (49)

    Denemearce *dat sing* (51)

Dene *masc pl noun*: the Danes (48)

dēor *neut noun*: wild beast, animals (26)

    dēor *acc pl* (26)

    dēora *gen pl* (25, 31)

durran *anom verb*: to dare

    dorston *3rd pers sing pret indic* (13, 15)

dȳre *adj*: dear, costly

    dȳre *nom pl* (28)

ēa *fem noun*: river (12, 13)

    ēas *gen sing* (13)

eahta *numeral*: eight (22)

eall *adj and adv*: all (13, 14)

    eal *nom sing masc* (4, 16, 35)

     ealle *acc sing fem* (44)

     ealne *acc sing masc* (6, 14, 45)

     ealra *gen pl* (1)

eardian *wk verb*: to dwell, live

     eardiað *pl pres indic* (36)

     eardodon *pl pret indic* (50)

ēast *adv*: eastwards (9)

     ēasteweard *adj*: eastward (36, 37)

     ēastryhte *adv*: eastward (9)

eln *fem noun*: ell (an historical measure of length that varied in meaning in different places and times, but here probably equivalent to Latin *cubitus* and somewhere in the range of 45 to 55 cm.)

     elna *gen pl* (21, 22, 33)

emnlange *prep with dat*: along (35)

Engle *masc pl noun*: the Angles (50)

erian *wk verb*: to plough (35)

     erede *3rd pers sing pret indic* (29)

ettan *wk verb*: to graze (35)

fandian *wk verb*: to try, examine, explore, experience (4)

faran *str verb*: to set forth, go, travel, wander, proceed

     faraþ *pl pres indic* (7)

     fōr *3rd pers sing pret indic* (5, 8, 14, 19)

feallan *str verb*: fall, extend

     fylð *3rd pers sing pres indic* (46)

fēawa *adj*: few

     fēawum *dat pl* (3)

fel *neut noun*: skin, hide (33)

fela *pron*: many (17, 49)

fell *acc pl* (33)

     fellum *dat pl* (31)

feor *adv*: far (7, 8)

     firrest *superl*: farthest (7)

fēower *numeral*: four (9)

fēowertiġes *numeral gen*: forty (22)

fersc *adj*: fresh

     fersce *nom pl* (40)

feðer *fem noun*: feather

     feðerum *dat pl* (31)

feðra *gen pl* (33)

fif *numeral:* five (11, 33, 48)

fiftiġes *numeral gen:* fifty (22)

fiftȳne *numeral:* fifteen (33)

Finn *masc noun:* "Finn," but probably actually referring to members of the
Sámi aboriginal peoples, whose languages are related to Finnish

Finnas *nom/acc pl* (3, 14, 18, 30, 36)

Finnum *dat pl* (28)

firrest: see feor

fiscaþ *masc noun:* fishing

fiscaþe *dat sing* (3)

fiscere *masc noun:* fisherman

fisceras *nom pl* (16)

fiscerum *dat pl* (14)

fōn *str verb:* take, seize, capture

fōð *pl pres indic* (28)

for *prep with dat:* for, because of, before (13, 19)

fōr: see faran

forþ *adv:* forth, forwards, onwards, further (13)

forþǣm, forðǣm *conj:* because (10, 13, 17, 19, 28)

from, fram *prep with dat:* from, by (14, 49)

fugel *masc noun:* bird (31)

fugela *gen pl* (31)

fugelere *masc noun:* fowler, bird-catcher

fugeleras *nom pl* (16)

fugelerum *dat pl* (14)

fyrst *superl adj:* first, most important

fyrstum *dat pl* (29)

gafol *neut noun:* tax, tribute (31)

gafole *dat sing* (30)

ġeond *prep with acc:* throughout (40)

ġiet, ġȳt *adv:* yet, still (8, 25)

gōd *adj:* good (20)

Gotland *neut noun:* Jutland (46, 49)

ġyf *conj:* if (44)

ġyldan *str verb:* to pay, yield (33)

ġyldað *pl pres indic* (30)

ġylt *3rd pers sing pres indic* (32)

ġȳt: see ġiet

habban *wk verb*: to have, hold
    habbaš *pl pres indic* (19, 40)
    hæfde *3rd pers sing pret indic* (25, 44)
    hæfdon *pl pret indic* (15)
    næfde *3rd pers sing pret indic*: did not have (29)
hǣt: see **hātan**
(æt) Hǣþum *prop noun*: Hedeby, a trading port on the Baltic Sea side of the
    Jutland peninsula (now in Schleswig, Germany) (48, 49)
Halgoland *prop noun*: a district of ancient Norway probably more extensive
    than the modern Norwegian province of Halogaland (41)
hām *masc noun*: home
    hām *dat sing* (14)
hātan *str verb*: to order, command, name, call
    hǣt *3rd pers sing pres indic* (43, 48)
    hātaš *pl pres indic* (26)
    hātte *3rd pers sing pres subj* (41)
hē *3rd pers personal pron*: he (1, etc.)
    hīe, hī, hȳ *nom/acc pl*: her, they, them (13, 15, 17, 19, 20, 26, 28,
        39, 40, 50)
    him, hym *masc/neut dat sing; dat pl*: him, to him; them, to them
        (6, 14, 18, 30, 42, 44, 49, 51)
    hira, hiera, hiora, heora, hyra *gen pl*: their (15, 17, 19, 20, 24, 30,
        40)
    his, hys *masc/neut gen sing*: his, its (1, 14, 22, 32, 35)
    hit *neut acc sing*: it (3, 17, 37)
healf *fem noun*: half, side
    healfe *dat sing* (13, 38, 46)
herġian *wk verb*: to ravage, plunder, raid
    herġiaš *pl pres indic* (39, 40)
hī: see **hē**
hider *adv*: hither, here (50)
hīe, hiera, him, hira, his, hit: see **hē**
hlāford *masc noun*: lord, master
    hlāforde *dat sing* (1)
hrān *masc noun*: reindeer
    hrānas *acc pl* (26, 28)
    hrānes *gen sing* (33)

hors *neut noun*: horse
    horsan *dat pl* (29)
horshwæl *masc noun*: walrus (literally, "horse-whale")
    horshwælum *dat pl* (19)
hrȳðer *neut noun*: cow, bull, steer
    hrȳðera *gen pl*: cattle (29)
hū *adv*: how (4)
hund *numeral*: hundred (25, 47)
hunta *masc noun*: hunter
    huntan *nom pl* (16)
    huntum *dat pl* (14)
huntoþ *masc noun*: hunting
    huntoþe *dat sing* (3)
hwæl *neut noun*: whale (referring to the "horse-whale" or walrus) (21)
    hwalas *nom pl* (20)
    hwales, hwæles *gen sing* (31, 33)
hwælhunta *masc noun*: whale-hunter
    hwælhuntan *nom pl* (7)
hwælhuntað *masc noun*: whale-fishing (22)
hwæt *pron*: what (17)
hwæðer *conj*: whether (4)
    hwæþer, hwæþer *pron*: which (of two) (9, 10)
hwalas, hwales: see **hwæl**
hwene *adv*: a little, somewhat (37)
hwīl *fem noun*: time, while
    hwīle *acc sing* (44)
    hwīlum *dat pl*: sometimes (39)
hwōn *adv*: a little (9)
hȳ: see **hē**
hȳd *fem noun*: hide (20)
    hȳde *dat sing* (31, 33)
hyra: see **hē**
hȳran *wk verb*: to obey
    hȳrð in on *3rd pers sing pres indic*: belongs to (48)
    in ... hȳrað *pl pres indic*: belong to ... (51)
hys: see **hē**

īġland *neut noun*: island
> **īġland** *nom pl* (44, 51)
> **īġlanda** *gen pl* (49)

in *prep with dat or acc*: in, into (9, etc.)

Īraland *neut noun*: Ireland (44)
> **Īralande** *dat sing* (44)

is: see **bēon**

kyrtel *masc noun*: kirtle, coat, tunic (33)

læġ, læġe: see **licgan**

lǣssa *adj compar*: less, smaller (21)

lǣtan *str verb*: to let, allow, leave
> **lēt** *3rd pers sing pret indic* (6)

land, lond *neut noun, nom/acc sing/pl*: land, country (3, etc.)
> **lande** *dat sing* (2, etc.)
> **landes** *gen sing* (19)
> **landum** *dat pl* (17, 50)

lang *adj*: long (3, 21, 33)
> **lange** *nom pl masc* (22)
> **lengra** *adj compar* (21)

lēohte *adj*: light (40)

lēt: see **lǣtan**

licgan *str verb*: to lie, extend
> **læġ** *3rd pers sing pret indic* (12)
> **læġe** *3rd pers sing pret subj* (4)
> **licgað** *pl pres indic* (35)
> **līð** *3rd pers sing pres indic* (35, 47)

lond: see **land**

longe *adv*: long, for a long time, far (6)

lytle *adj*: little (29, 40)

mā *compar adv*: more (29)
> **mǣst** *superl adj*: most (30)
> **mǣstan** *acc pl masc*: largest (22)

mæġ, mæġe: see **magan**

mǣniġ *adj*: many (29)

mǣst, mǣstan: see **mā**

magan *wk verb*: can; to be able, be competent

mæġ *3rd pers sing pres indic* (35, 37)

mæġe *3rd pers sing pres subj* (46)

meahte, mehte, mihte *3rd pers sing pret indic/subj*: might (8, 9, 11, 37, 44)

man, mon *masc noun*: person, man (4, 24, 46); *as indef pron*: one (35, 37, 42, 43, 44, 48)

mannum *dat pl* (29)

meahte: see **magan**

mearð *masc noun*: marten

mearðes *gen sing* (33)

mehte: see **magan**

mere *masc noun*: mere, lake, sea

meras *nom/acc pl* (40)

metan *wk verb*: to meet, encounter

mette *3rd pers sing pret indic* (14)

miċel, myċel *adj*: great, big, large (12, 46)

miċle *adv*: much (21); *adj nom pl masc*: large (40)

mid *prep with dat*: with, among (28, 29)

middeweard *adj*: toward the middle (37)

mīla *fem noun, gen pl*: miles (37, 47)

mon: see **man**

mōnað *masc noun*: month

mōnðe *dat sing* (44)

mōr *masc noun*: moor, mountainous region (37, 39)

mōras *acc pl* (35, 40)

mōre *dat sing* (37)

mōres *gen sing* (38)

mōrum *dat pl* (36)

myċel: see **miċel**

næfde: see **habban**

nān *adj*: none, not one, not any, no (14, 42)

ne *adv/conj*: not, nor (13, 14, 15, 17, 21, 42, 44)

nēah *adv*: near, almost, nearly (18)

niht *fem noun*: night (44)

norþ *adv*: north (3, 7)

norþan *adj*: northerly; from the north (9)

be norþan *prep with dat*: to the north of (4)

norðeweard *adj*: northward (37, 38)

norþ(e)weardum *dat sing* (2, 38)

Norðman *masc noun*: Norwegian
    Norðmen *nom/acc pl* (35, 36, 39, 40)
    Norþmonna, Norðmanna *gen pl* (1, 30, 34)
norþmest *adv superl*: northmost (1)
norðor *adv compar*: more northerly (36)
norþryhte *adv*: northwards; to the north (4, 5, 8)
norþweardum: see norþeweard
Norðwēġ *prop noun*: Norway (45)
nysse, nyste: see witan

of *prep with dat*: of, from, among, concerning (17, 31, 33, 48)
ofer *prep with acc and adv*: over, across (39, 40, 46)
oferfēran *wk verb*: to traverse (37)
ofslēan *str verb*: kill
    ofslōge *3rd pers sing pret subj* (23)
Ohthere *prop noun*: Ohthere (1, 41)
on *prep with acc or dat*: on, onto, upon, in, into, against (2, 3, etc.)
onġēan *adv*: opposite (46)
oþ *prep with acc and conj*: until, up to, as far as (38, 45)
ōþer *adj/pron*: other, another, next, remaining
    ōþre *dat sing fem, nom pl masc* (13, 21, 38, 46)
    ōþrum *dat pl* (8)
ōþer ... ōþer ... *correl conj*: one ... the other ... (33)
oþþe, oððe *conj*: or (4, 9, 10, 16, 33, 37)

port *masc noun*: port, harbour (43)
    porte *dat sing* (48)

ryhtnorþanwind *masc noun*: a wind from due north
    ryhtnorþanwindes *gen sing* (10)

sǣ *fem/masc noun*: sea (3, 9, 10, 35, 46, 47)
sǣde, sǣdon: see secgan
sceal(l): see sculan
scēapa *neut noun*: sheep
    scēapa *gen pl* (29)
scēawung *fem noun*: seeing, surveying
    scēawunge *dat sing* (19)

sceolde: see sculan

scipráp *masc noun*: ship-rope, cable

> sciprápas *acc pl* (33)
>
> sciprápum *dat pl* (20, 31)

scír *fem noun*: shire, district, division (41)

Scíringesheal *prop name*: Skiringssalr, identified by a recent archaeological team as the trading port excavated at Kaupang, Norway (43)

> Scírin(c)gesheale *dat sing* (45, 46, 48, 49)

sculan *anom verb*: must, ought to, have to, shall

> sceal(l) *3rd pers sing pres indic* (33, 44)
>
> sceolde *3rd pers sing pret indic* (10)

scyp *neut noun*: ship

scypu, scypa *acc pl* (40)

se *dem pron*: the, that (21, etc.)

> séo, sío *nom sing fem* (9, 10, 41, 46, 47)
>
> þá *acc sing fem* (2, etc.); *nom/acc pl* (7, etc.)
>
> þæm *dat sing masc/neut* (2, etc.); *dat pl* (8, etc.)
>
> þære *dat/gen sing fem* (3, 13)
>
> þæs *gen sing masc/neut* (17, 19, 38)
>
> þæt, ðæt *nom/acc sing neut* (3, etc.)
>
> þára *gen pl* (16, 23, 27)
>
> þone *acc sing masc* (25, 39, 43, 46)

Seaxe *pl noun*: the Saxons, Saxony

> Seaxum *dat* (48)

ġeseah: see séon

sécan *wk verb*: visit

> sóhte *3rd pers sing pret indic* (25)

secgan *wk verb*: to say, tell

> sæde *3rd pers sing pret indic* (1, 3, 6, 41, 59, 80)
>
> sædon *pl pret indic* (31)

seġlian, ġeseġlian, seġlode: see siġlan

self *pron*: self, himself (31)

séo: see se

séolh, síolh *masc noun*: seal

> séoles, síoles *gen sing* (31, 33)

séon *str verb*: to see, look (46)

> ġeseah *3rd pers sing pret indic* (17)

síe: see béon

ġesiġlan, ġeseġlian *wk verb*: to sail (8, 9, 11, 13, 44)

seġlode *3rd pers sing pret indic* (48, 49)
    siġlde *3rd pers sing pret indic* (9, 11)
Sillende *prop name*: Zealand (46, 49)
sint: see **bēon**
sīo: see **se**
sīolh, sīoles: see **sēolh**
siþþan, siððan, syðþan *conj or adv*: after, since, when; afterwards (14, 37, 46)
smæl *adj*: small, narrow (34)
    smǣlre *compar* (36)
    smālost *superl* (37)
sōhte: see **sēcan**
sōþ *neut noun*: truth
    sōþes *gen sing* (17)
spēd *fem noun*: success, wealth
    spēda *nom pl*: (24)
spēdiġ *adj*: prosperous, rich, powerful (24)
spell *neut noun*: story
    spella *gen pl* (17)
sprēcan *str verb*: speak
    sprǣcon *verb pl pret indic*: spoke (18)
stælhrān *masc noun*: decoy reindeer
    stælhrānas *nom pl* (27)
standan *str verb*: stand
    stent *3rd pers sing pres indic* (48)
stēorbord *neut noun*: starboard, right hand side of a ship (6, 14, 44, 49)
stōw *fem noun*: place
    stōwum *dat pl* (3, 35, 37)
styċċemǣlum *adv*: in pieces, bit by bit, piecemeal, here and there (3)
sum *adj and pron*: some, a certain (23)
    sume *acc sing masc* (20)
    sumum *dat sing masc; dat pl* (4, 35, 37)
sumer *masc noun*: summer
    sumera *dat sing* (3)
sūþryhte *adv*: southwards (10, 11)
sūðweardum *adj*: southward (38, 43)
swā ... swā *correl adv and conj*: so ... as; as ... as; so much the more ... so
    much the more (7, 8, 36, 37)
swā swā: *conj*: so as; as much as (9, 11)
Swēoland *prop name*: Sweden (38)

swīþe, swȳ̌ðe *adv*: very, exceedingly (3, 15, 19, 20, 24, 28, 34, 35, 40, 46)
      swīþost *adv superl* (19)
swȳn *neut noun*: swine, hog
      swȳna *gen pl* (29)
sȳ: see **bēon**
syfan *numeral*: seven (21)
symle *adv*: ever, always (36)
synd: see **bēon**
syðþan: see **siþþan**
syx *numeral*: six (25, 27, 37)
      syxa sum as one of six (i.e., with five others) (23)
syxtiġ *numeral*: sixty (23, 33, 37)

tam *adj*: tame
tamra *gen pl* (25)
Terfinn *prop name*: a Ter Sámi, one of the aboriginal inhabitants of the
    Kola Peninsula
      Terfinna *gen pl* (16)
tōð *masc noun*: tooth
      tēð *acc pl* (20)
      tōþum *dat pl* (19)
tō *prep with dat*: to, at, for; *adv*: too (20, 45, 48, 49)
tōēacan *conj*: in addition to (19)
tōemnes *prep with dat*: alongside (38)
twā *numeral*: two
      twām *dat pl* (23, 37)
      twēġen *acc pl* (33, 49, 51)
twentiġ *numeral*: twenty (29)
tȳn *numeral*: ten (33)

þā, ðā *conj*: then, at that time, when (5, etc.)
      þā ġiet, þā ġȳt *adv*: still (8, 25)
þā, þǣm, þǣre, þāra: see **se**
þǣr, ðǣr *adv/conj*: there, where (9, 10, 12, 16, 37, 40)
þǣron *adv*: therein (15)
þǣs: see **se**
þæt *conj*: that, so that (1, 2, 3, 4, 9, 23, 34, 40, 42, 48)
þanon: see **þonan**
þe *rel pron*: that, which (17, 24, 30, 31, 41, 48, 51)

þēah *adv*: however, yet (3, 29, 35)
ġeþēode *neut noun*: language (18)
ðider, þyder *adv*: thither, (to) there (19, 44)
þiderweard *adv*: thitherwards, towards that place (49)
þis *dem pron*: this (45)
        þissum *dat sing* (44)
þonan, þanon *adv*: from that time or place, away (3, 11, 40)
þonne *adv*: then, when (38, 43, 44, 45); *compar*: than (21, 29, 46)
þrīe, þrȳ *numeral*: three (6, 49)
        þrēora *gen* (37)
        þrīm *dat* (8)
þrītiġ *numeral*: thirty (37)
þyncan *wk verb*: seem
        þuhte *3rd pers sing pret indic* (18)
þyder: see ðider

unbeboht *adj*: unsold
        unbebohtra *gen pl* (25)
unfriþ *masc noun*: hostility, violence
        unfriþe *dat sing* (13)
up in on *prep with acc*: up into (13, 14, 46, 47)
ūtan *adv*: outside (17)

wæs, wǣre, wǣron: see bēon
wēġ *masc noun*: way (6, 14, 45)
wel *adv*: well (15)
westan *adj*: from the west (9)
wēste *adj*: waste, barren, desolate, uninhabited, empty (3, 6, 14, 16)
wēsten *masc noun*: desert, wilderness
        wēstenne *dat sing* (4)
Westsǣ *fem noun*: Western Sea, i.e., North Atlantic (2)
wīcian *wk verb*: to dwell, lodge, camp
        wīciaþ *pl pres indic* (4)
        ġewīcodon *pl pret indic* (16)
        wīcode *3rd pers sing pret indic*: camped? rode at anchor? (44)
wīdsǣ *fem noun*: open sea, ocean (6, 14, 49)
wilde *adj*: wild
        wildan *acc pl masc* (28)
        wilde *nom pl masc* (35)

wilddēor *neut noun*: wild beast (here, especially reindeer)
      wildrum *dat pl* (24)
willan *wk verb*: to wish, desire, will
      wolde *3rd pers sing pret indic*: wanted to (4)
wind *masc noun*: wind (44)
      windes *gen sing* (9)
Wīnedum *dat pl*: the Wends (48)
winter *masc noun*: winter
      wintra *dat sing* (3)
witan *anom verb*: to know, to understand, to be aware of
      wisse *3rd pers sing pret indic* (9)
      nysse, nyste *3rd pers sing pret indic*: did not know (9, 10, 17)
wiþ, wið *prep with acc*: against, along, in return for, from, with (2, 35, 46)
      wiþ ēastan to the east (35)
      wiþ sūðan to the south of (46)
      wið uppon *adv* above (35)
wolde: see **willan**
ġeworht: see **ġewyrcan**
wucu *fem noun*: week
      wucum *dat pl* (37)
ġewyrcan *wk verb*: to make, produce, create
      ġeworht *past part*: made (31, 33)

ymb ... utan *adv*: about, around (17)
yterenne *adj*: made of otter skin (33)

Aelfric's Colloquy

Introduction

Ælfric of Eynsham "the grammarian" was abbot first of Cerne and then, from 1005, of Eynsham, and lived approximately from 955 to 1010. He was a prolific author in Latin and Old English; his Old English homilies and saints' lives are among the most admired prose works of the period.

The *Colloquy* is a humbler production. Ælfric wrote it in Latin as a dialogue for young monks and novices to use to practise that language, which they had to learn in order to take part in the life of the abbey. Some time later another teacher added an Old English gloss to one manuscript of the *Colloquy* between the lines of the Latin, and it is that Old English crib which is presented here.

While it is by no means exactly known what classroom use would have been made of the *Colloquy*, it is reasonable to assume that the pupils would learn the individual speeches, perhaps taking the part of one or other of the characters; the presence of the gloss suggests that they would also be responsible for translation into Old English of the Latin text. The *Colloquy* is presented here as if used in the classroom as a play to be read aloud, with each of the novices (identified as Pupil A, and so on) taking a different part.

The *Colloquy* has a loose dramatic structure. After a brief introductory section in which the students ask for instruction, the fiction of the first part (from 8 to 127) is that the members of the class are practitioners of the different occupations of Anglo-Saxon village and town life (a plowman, a hunter, a merchant, a leatherworker, and so on), who are interrogated by the teacher on the nature and practices of their various professions. Their conversation degenerates into an argument about social utility, settled by the teacher in consultation with a ruler or "wise counsellor." In a second, framing part (128 to the end), the boys are asked about their daily life as young members of the monastic community. Each section ends with a speech of moral instruction by the teacher, the first preaching concord to the trades, the second dignified behaviour to the novices.

Humble as it is as a literary production, the *Colloquy* is a valued and much-cited historical document because of the glimpses it gives us of daily life in Anglo-Saxon England, filtered as they are through the pedagogical purpose of instruction in grammar and vocabulary. Because of the elite place of literacy during the period, we have little in the form of text (as opposed to archaeological evidence, now becoming a very impressive source of knowledge) from which we can glean much information about the lives of the common people, especially, and although the *Colloquy* itself springs from a monastic environment that may itself constitute a kind of information-filter, it does at least paint a picture of life among the less eminent members of society.

It is somehow fitting to use this text, designed for language instruction about a thousand years ago, to learn Old English. Presumably Ælfric set the dialogue among plowmen and fishermen to appeal to his boys' familiar lived experience and arouse their interest; paradoxically, the text arouses our interest by opening a window onto what is for us an unfamiliar and distant world.

The text presented here closely follows that of the manuscript, with a very few silent emendations to correct mistranslations of the Latin and to fill gaps in the gloss.

Aelfric's *Colloquy*

1 [The pupils:] Wē ċildra biddaþ þē, ēalā lārēow, þæt þū tǣce ūs sprecan, forþām unġelǣrede wē syndon and ġewæmodlīċe wē sprecaþ.

2 [The teacher:] Hwæt wille ġē sprecan?

3 [The pupils:] Hwæt rēċe wē hwæt wē sprecan, būton hit riht sprǣċ sȳ and behēfe, næs īdel oþþe fracod.

4 [The teacher:] Wille ġē bēon beswungen on leornunge?

5 [The pupils:] Lēofre ys ūs bēon beswungen for lāre þænne hit ne cunnan. Ac wē witun þē bilewitne wesan and nellan onbelǣden swincgla ūs,[1] būton þū bī tōgenȳdd fram ūs.[2]

6 [The teacher:] Iċ āxie þē, hwæt sprycst þū?[3] Hwæt hæfst þū weorkes?[4]

7 [Pupil A:] Iċ eom ġeanwyrde monuc,[5] and sincge ælċe dæġ seofon tīda[6] mid ġebroþrum, ond iċ eom bysgod on sange, ac þēahhwæþere iċ wolde betwēnan leornian sprecan on lēden ġereorde.

8 [The teacher:] Hwæt cunnon þās þīne ġefēran?[7]

9 [Pupil A:] Summe synt yrþlincgas, sume scēphyrdas, sume oxanhyrdas, sume ēac swylce huntan, sume fisceras, sume fugleras, sume cȳpmenn, sume scēwyrhtan, sealteras, bæceras.

10 [The teacher:] Hwæt sæġest þū, yrþlingc? Hū begæst þū weorc þīn?

11 [Pupil B:] Ēalā, lēof hlāford, þearle iċ deorfe. Iċ gā ūt on dæġrǣd þȳwende oxan tō felda, ond iugie hīġ tō sȳl. Nys hit swā stearc winter þæt iċ durre[8] lūtian æt hām for eġe hlāfordes mīnes, ac ġeiukodan oxan, ond ġefæstnodon sceare ond cultre mid þǣre sȳl,[9] ælċe dæġ iċ sceal erian fulne æcer oþþe māre.

12 [The teacher:] Hæfst þū æniġne ġefēran?

---

1 **nellan onbelǣden swincgla ūs:** "not to want to beat us."

2 **tōgenȳdd fram ūs:** "forced by us."

3 **hwæt sprycst þū:** a somewhat mysterious question even in the Latin original. Perhaps "What do you have to say for yourself" or "What are you going to say to me."

4 **Hwæt hæfst þū weorkes?:** "What (kind) of work do you have?"

5 **ġeanwyrde monuc:** a monk who has taken monastic vows.

6 **seofon tīda:** the seven canonical "hours" or required monastic sung services (matins, lauds, prime, tierce, sext, none, and vespers), six of which are listed below at 139.

7 **Hwæt cunnon þās þīne ġefēran?:** "What do these companions of yours know how to do?"

8 **Nys hit swā stearc winter þæt iċ durre:** i.e., "there is no winter so cold that I dare."

9 **ġeiukodan oxan ... mid þǣre sȳl:** "with the oxen yoked and the share and coulter fastened to the plow." The medieval plow consisted of a wooden beam to which were fastened two separate iron blades that cut the soil vertically (the coulter) and sliced it horizontally while turning it over (the share).

13 [Pupil B:] Iċ hæbbe sumne cnapan þȳwende oxan mid gādīsene, þe ēac swilce nū hās ys for cylde ond hrēame.

14 [The teacher:] Hwæt māre dēst þū on dæġ?

15 [Pupil B:] Ġewyslīċe māre iċ dō. Iċ sceal fyllan binne oxena mid hīġ, ond wæterian hīġ, ond scearn heora beran ūt.

16 [The teacher:] Hīġ! Hīġ! Miċel ġedeorf ys hit!

17 [Pupil B:] Ġēa lēof, miċel ġedeorf hit is, forþām iċ neom frēoh.[10]

18 [The teacher:] Sċēaphyrde, hæfst þū æniġ ġedeorf?

19 [Pupil C:] Ġēa, lēof, iċ hæbbe. On forewerdne morġen iċ drīfe sċēap mīne to heora læse ond stande ofer hīġ on hæte ond on cyle mid hundum, þȳ læs wulfas forswelġen hīġ, ond iċ āġēnlæde hīġ on heora loca, ond melke hīġ tweowa on dæġ, ond heora loca iċ hæbbe, ond þærtō ġe ċȳse ġe buteran iċ dō, ond iċ eom ġetrȳwe hlāforde mīnum.

20 [The teacher:] Ēalā, oxanhyrde, hwæt wyrcst þū?

21 [Pupil D:] Ēalā, hlāford mīn, miċel iċ ġedeorfe. Þænne se yrthlingc unscenþ þā oxan, ic læde hīġ tō læse, ond ealle niht iċ stande ofer hīġ waciende for þēofum, ond eft on ærnemerġen iċ betæċe hīġ þæm yrþlincge wel ġefylde ond ġewæterode.

22 [The teacher:] Is þæs of þīnum ġefērum?[11]

23 [Pupil A:] Ġēa, hē is.

24 [The teacher:] Canst þū[12] æniġ þing?

25 [Pupil E:] Ænne cræft iċ cann.

26 [The teacher:] Hwylċne?

27 [Pupil E:] Hunta iċ eom.

28 [The teacher:] Hwæs?

29 [Pupil E:] Cincges.

30 [The teacher:] Hū begæst þū cræft þīnne?

31 [Pupil E:] Iċ brēde mē max ond sette hīġ on stōwe ġehæppre, ond ġetihte hundas mīne þæt wildēor hīġ ēhton, oþþæt hīġ becuman tō þæm nettum unforsċēawodlīċe ond þæt hīġ swā bēon begrȳnodo, ond iċ ofslēa hīġ on þæm maxum.

32 [The teacher:] Ne canst þū huntian būton mid nettum?

33 [Pupil E:] Ġēa, būtan nettum huntian iċ mæġ.

34 [The teacher:] Hū?

---

10 **neom frēoh**: slaves occupied the lowest positions in the Anglo-Saxon social hierarchy and did menial labour.

11 **Is þæs of þīnum ġefērum?**: "Is this (one) of your companions?"

12 **Canst þū**: "do you know how to do."

35 [Pupil E:] Mid swiftum hundum iċ betǣċe[13] wildēor.

36 [The teacher:] Hwilċe wildēor swȳþost ġefēhst þū?

37 [Pupil E:] Iċ ġefēo heortas ond bāras ond rānn ond rǣgan ond hwīlon haran.

38 [The teacher:] Wǣre þū tōdæġ on huntnoþe?

39 [Pupil E:] Iċ næs, forþām sunnandæġ is, ac ġyrstandæġ iċ wæs on huntunge.

40 [The teacher:] Hwæt ġelæhtest þū?

41 [Pupil E:] Twēġen heortas ond ænne bār.

42 [The teacher:] Hū ġefencge þū hīġ?

43 [Pupil E:] Heortas iċ ġefencge on nettum ond bār ic ofslōh.

44 [The teacher:] Hū wǣre þū dyrstiġ ofstikian bār?

45 [Pupil E:] Hundas bedrīfon hine tō mē, ond iċ þær tōġēanes standende fǣrlīċe ofstikode hine.

46 [The teacher:] Swȳþe þrȳste wǣre þū þā!

47 [Pupil E:] Ne sceal hunta forhtfull wesan, forþām mislīċe wildēor wuniaþ on wudum.

48 [The teacher:] Hwæt dēst þū be þīnre huntunge?

49 [Pupil E:] Iċ sylle cyncge swā hwæt swā ic gefō, forþām iċ eom hunta his.

50 [The teacher:] Hwæt sylþ hē þē?

51 [Pupil E:] Hē scrȳt mē wel ond fētt ond hwīlon sylþ me hors oþþe bēah, þæt þē lustlicor cræft mīnne iċ begancge.

52 [The teacher:] Hwylċne cræft canst þū?

53 [Pupil F:] Iċ eom fiscere.

54 [The teacher:] Hwæt beġyst þū of þīnum cræfte?

55 [Pupil F:] Bīġleofan ond scrūd ond feoh.

56 [The teacher:] Hū gefehst þū fixas?

57 [Pupil :] Iċ āstiġie mīn scyp ond wyrpe max mīne on ēa, ond ancgil iċ wyrpe ond spyrtan, ond swā hwæt swā hīġ ġehæftað iċ ġenime.

58 [The teacher:] Hwæt ġif hī unclǣne bēoþ fixas?[14]

---

13 betǣċe: a mysterious gloss for Latin "insequor" ("pursue"), since the word normally means "hand over, entrust, bestow," as at 21; possibly an error, though "show, point" has been suggested, that is, the dogs help to locate the game.

14 unclǣne ... fixas: Presumably a reference to Mosaic law, according to which fish without scales and fins were unclean and not to be eaten (Leviticus 11: 9-10; Deuteronomy 14: 9-10). This prohibition is understood by rabbinic scholars as extending to shellfish as well as to fish without visible scales, such as the shark, sturgeon, and freshwater eel. Since eels, sturgeons, and shellfish are all mentioned as the fisherman's catches, it is not clear how the term "unclean" is being understood here.

59 [Pupil F:] Iċ ūtwyrpe þā unclǣnan ūt, ond ġenime mē clǣne tō mete.
60 [The teacher:] Hwǣr ċȳpst þū fixas þīne?
61 [Pupil F:] On ċeastre.
62 [The teacher:] Hwā biġþ hī?
63 [Pupil F:] Ċeasterwara. Iċ ne mæġ swā fela ġefōn swā iċ mæġ ġesyllan.
64 [The teacher:] Hwilċe fixas ġefēhst þū?
65 [Pupil F:] Ǣlas ond hacodas, mynas ond ǣlepūtan, sceotan ond lampredan, ond swā wylċe swā on wætere swymmaþ.
66 [The teacher:] Forhwī ne fixast þū on sǣ?
67 [Pupil F:] Hwīlum iċ dō, ac seldon, forþām miċel rēwyt mē ys tō sǣ.
68 [The teacher:] Hwæt fēhst þū on sǣ?
69 [Pupil F:] Hǣrincgas ond leaxas, mereswȳn ond stirian, ostran ond crabban, muslan, winewinclan, sǣcoccas, fagc ond floc ond lopystran ond fela swylces.
70 [The teacher:] Wilt þū fōn sumne[15] hwæl?
71 [Pupil F:] Niċ.
72 [The teacher:] Forhwī?
73 [Pupil F:] Forþām plyhtlic þingc hit ys ġefōn hwæl. Ġebeorhliċre ys mē faran tō ēa mid scype mȳnum, þænne faran mid manegum scypum on huntunge hranes.
74 [The teacher:] Forhwī swā?
75 [Pupil F:] Forþām lēofre ys mē ġefōn fisc þæne[16] iċ mæġ ofslēan, þonne fisc, þe nā þæt ān mē ac ēac swylce mīne ġefēran mid ānum sleġe hē mæġ besenċean oþþe ġecwylman.
76 [The teacher:] Ond þēah mæniġe ġefōþ hwælas, ond ætberstaþ frēċnysse, ond miċelne sceat þanon beġytaþ.
77 [Pupil F:] Sōþ þū seġst, ac iċ ne ġeþristġe for mōdes mīnes nytenyssæ.
78 [The teacher:] Hwæt sæġst þū, fugelere? Hū beswīcst þū fugelas?
79 [Pupil G:] On feala wīsan iċ beswīċe fugelas: hwīlum mid netum, hwīlum mid grīnum, hwīlum mid līme, hwīlum mid hwistlunge, hwīlum mid hafoce, hwīlum mid treppum.
80 [The teacher:] Hæfst þū hafoc?
81 [Pupil G:] Iċ hæbbe.
82 [The teacher:] Canst þū temian hiġ?
83 [Pupil G:] Ġēa, iċ cann. Hwæt sceoldon hiġ mē[17] būton iċ cūþe temian hiġ?

15 **sumne**: translate "a (whale)."
16 **þæne**: acts as a relative pronoun here: translate "that, which."
17 **Hwæt sceoldon hiġ mē**: "What use would they be to me."

84 [The teacher:] Sylle mē ǣnne hafoc.

85 [Pupil G:] Iċ sylle lustlīċe, ġyf þū sylst mē ǣnne swiftne hund. Hwilċne hafoc wilt þū habban, þone māran hwæþer þe þænne lǣssan?

86 [The teacher:] Syle mē þæne māran.

87 [The teacher:] Hū āfēst þū hafocas þīne?

88 [Pupil G:] Hīġ fēdaþ hīġ sylfe ond mē on wintra, ond on lencgten iċ lǣte hīġ ætwindan to wuda, ond ġenyme mē briddas on hærfæste, ond temiġe hīġ.

89 [The teacher:] Ond forhwī forlǣst þū þā ġetemedon ætwindan fram þē?

90 [Pupil G:] Forþām iċ nelle fēdan hīġ on sumera, forþām þe hīġ þearle etaþ.

91 [The teacher:] Ond maniġe fēdaþ þā ġetemodon ofer sumor, þæt eft hīġ hīġ habban ġearuwe.

92 [Pupil G:] Ġēa, swā hīġ dōþ, ac iċ nelle swā deorfan ofer hīġ, forþām iċ cann ōþre, nā þæt ān ǣnne, ac ēac swilċe maniġe ġefōn.

93 [The teacher:] Hwæt sæġst þū, mancgere?

94 [Pupil H:] Iċ secge þæt behēfe iċ eom ġe cyngce ond ealdormannum ond weliġum ond eallum follce.

95 [The teacher:] Ond hū?

96 [Pupil H:] Iċ āstige mīn scyp mid hlæstum mīnum, ond rōwe ofer sǣlīċe dǣlas, ond ċȳpe mīne þingc, ond bicge dȳrwyrþe þingc þā[18] on þisum lande ne bēoþ ācennede ond iċ hit tōġelǣde ēow hider mid micċlan plihte ofer sǣ, ond hwīlum forlidenesse iċ þolie mid lyre ealra þinga mīnra, unēaþe cwic ætberstende.

97 [The teacher:] Hwilce þinc[19] ġelǣdst þū ūs?

98 [Pupil H:] Pællas ond sīdan, dēorwyrþe ġymmas ond gold, selcūþe rēaf ond wyrtġemangc, wīn ond ele, ylpesbān ond mæstlingc, ǣr ond tin, swefel ond glæs, ond þylċes fela.[20]

99 [The teacher:] Wilt þū syllan þingc þīne hēr eal swā[21] þū hī ġebohtest þǣr?

100 [Pupil H:] Iċ nelle. Hwæt þænne mē fremode ġedeorf mīn? Ac iċ wille heora ċȳpen hēr dēoror þonne ġebicge iċ hīġ þǣr, þæt sum ġestrēon iċ mē beġyte, þanon iċ mē āfēde ond mīn wīf ond mīnne sunu.

101 [The teacher:] Þū, sceōwyrhta, hwæt wyrcst þū ūs nytwyrþnessæ?

102 [Pupil I:] Is, witodlīċe, cræft mīn behēfe þearle ēow ond nēodþearf.

103 [The teacher:] Hū?

104 [Pupil I:] Iċ bicge hȳda ond fell, ond ġearkie hīġ mid cræfte mīnon, ond

18 þā: here used as a relative pronoun (translate "that" or "which").
19 Hwilce þinc: "What kinds of things."
20 þylċes fela: "many things like that."
21 eal swā: "just as"; i.e., "at the same price as."

wyrce of him ġescȳ mistliċes cynnes, swyftlēras ond sceōs, leþerhosa ond butericas, brīdelþwancgas ond ġerǣda, flaxan oþþe pinnan[22] ond hīġdifatu, spurleþera ond hælftra, pusan ond fætelsas; ond nān ēower nele oferwintran būton mīnon cræfte.

105 [The teacher:] Sealtere, hwæt ūs fremaþ cræft þīn?

106 [Pupil J:] Þearle fremaþ cræft mīn ēow eallum. Nān ēower blisse brȳcð on ġererduncge oþþe mete, būton cræft mīn gistlīþe him bēo.

107 [The teacher:] Hū?

108 [Pupil J:] Hwylc manna þurhwerodum þurhbrȳcþ mettum[23] būton swæcce sealtes? Hwā ġefylþ cleafan his oþþe hēdderna būton cræfte mīnon?[24] Efne, buterġeþwēor ælc ond cȳsgerunn losaþ ēow būton iċ hyrde ætwese[25] ēow, þe ne furþon þæt ān[26] wyrtum ēowrum būtan mē brūcaþ.

109 [The teacher:] Bæcere, hwām fremaþ cræft þīn oþþe hwæþer wē būtan þē magon līf ādrēogan?

110 [Pupil K:] Ġē magon þurh sum fæc būtan nā lancge ne tō wel: sōþlīċe būtan cræfte mīnon ælċ bēod æmtiġ byþ ġesewen,[27] ond būton hlāfe ælċ mete tō wlættan byþ ġehwyrfed.[28] Iċ heortan mannes ġestrangie, iċ eom mæġen wera ond furþon litlincgas nellaþ forbīġean mē.

111 [The teacher:] Hwæt secge wē be þæm cōcce? Hwæþer wē his cræft beþurfon on ænigon þinge?

112 [Pupil L:] Ġif ġē mē ūt ādrīfaþ fram ēowrum ġefērscype, ġē etaþ wyrta ēowre grēne, ond flæscmettas ēowre hrēawe, ond furþon fætt broþ[29] ġē ne magon būtan cræfte mīnum habban.

113 [A pupil:] Wē ne reċċaþ his cræftes[30] ne hē ūs nēodþearf ys, forþām wē sylfe magon sēoþan þā þingc þe tō sēoþenne synd, and brǣdan þā þincg þe tō brǣdenne synd.

---

22 flaxan and pinnan are alternative translations of a single Latin word.

23 þurhwerodum þurhbrȳcþ mettum: "really enjoys very sweet food" ("þurhwerodum" modifies "mettum").

24 Hwā ġefylþ ... : a reference to the use of salt in preserving meats and other foodstuffs.

25 būton iċ hyrde ætwese: "unless I am (i.e., the salt is) present as a keeper."

26 þe ne furþon þæt ān: "who not even."

27 æmtiġ byþ ġesewen: "is seen as empty."

28 tō wlættan byþ ġehwyrfed: "becomes disgusting."

29 fætt broþ: Since in this sentence the cook is proclaiming the general usefulness of his art in turning raw food into cooked food, this expression might be a reference to fatty or greasy broth made by simply boiling meat in water; more likely, the word fætt means "thick" here, and the dish in question is a simple household soup made of meat broth thickened with grain and perhaps vegetables, like Scotch broth.

30 ne reċċaþ his cræftes: "do not care about his craft."

114 [Pupil L:] Ġif ġē forþȳ mē fram ādrȳfaþ, þæt ġē þus dōn,³¹ þonne bēo ġē
ealle þrǣlas, ond nān ēower ne biþ hlāford; þēahhwæþere būton mē ġē ne etaþ.

115 [The teacher:] Ēalā, munuc, þe mē tōspycst, efne, iċ hæbbe āfandod þē
habban gōde ġefēran ond þearle nēodþearfe; ond iċ āhsie hwā þā synd?

116 [Pupil A:] Ic hæbbe smiþas, īsene smiþas, goldsmiþ, seoloforsmiþ, ārsmiþ,
trēowwyrhtan ond maneġra ōþre mistliċra cræfta bīggenceras.

117 [The teacher:] Hæfst ænigne wīsne ġeþeahtan?

118 [Pupil A:] Ġewislīċe iċ hæbbe. Hū meahte ūre ġegaderungc būton
ġeþeahtynde bēon wissod?

119 [The teacher:] Wīsa, hwilc cræft þē is ġeþuht³² betwux þās furþra wesan?

120 [Pupil M:] Mē is ġeþuht Godes þēowdōm betweoh þās cræftas ealdorscype
healdan, swā swā hit ġerǣd on godspelle: "Fyrmest seċeaδ rīċe Godes ond
rihtwīsnesse hys, ond þās þingc ealle bēoþ tōġehyhte ēow."³³

121 [The teacher:] Hwilc þē is ġeþuht betwux woruldcræftas heoldan ealdordōm?

122 [Pupil M:] Eorþtilþ, forþām sē yrþling ūs ealle fētt.³⁴

123 Sē smiþ seġδ: Hwanon sylan scear oþþe culter, þe nā gāde hæfþ būton of
cræfte mīnon? Hwanon fiscere ancgel, oþþe sceōwyrhton æl, oþþe sēamere
nǣdl? Nis hit of mīnon ġeweorce?

124 Sē ġeþeahtend ondsweraþ: Sōþ witodlīċe þū sæġst, ac eallum ūs lēofre ys
wīkian mid þē, yrþlincge, þonne mid þē, forþām sē yrþling sylδ ūs hlāf ond
drenc;³⁵ þū, hwæt sylst ūs on smiþþan þīnre būton īsenne fȳrspearcan ond
swēġincga bēatendra slecgea ond blāwendra byliga?

125 Sē trēowwyrhta seġδ: Hwilc ēower ne notaþ cræfte mīnon, þonne hūs ond
mistliċe fata ond scypa ēow eallum iċ wyrce?

126 Sē smiþ ondwyrt: Ēalā, trēowwyrhta, forhwī swā sprycst þū, þonne ne
furþon ān þyrl þū ne miht dōn būtan minum cræfte?

127 Sē ġeþeahtend sæġþ: Ēalā, ġefēran and gōde wyrhtan, uton tōwurpon
hwætlīcor þās ġeflitu, ond sȳ sibb ond ġeþwǣrnyss betweoh ūs, ond framiġe
ānra ġehwylċ ōþron on cræfte hys, and ġeδwǣrian symble mid þām yrþlinge,
þǣr wē bīġleofan ūs ond fōddor horsum ūrum habbaþ. Ond þis ġeþeaht ic sylle
eallum wyrhtum, þæt ānra ġehwylċ cræft his ġeornlīċe begange, forþām sē þe

---

31 **þæt ġē þus dōn**: "in order to do so," i.e., intending to do their own cooking.

32 **þē is ġeþuht**: "seems to you."

33 "But seek ye first the kingdom of God, and his righteousness; and all these things shall be
     added unto you" (Matthew 6: 33).

34 Proclaiming the plowman to have the leadership of the earthly crafts is a pious sentiment
     that seems not to have been in conflict in the medieval mind with the actual social position
     of plowmen.

35 **ond drenc**: i.e., by growing barley for beer-brewing.

cræft his forlæt, hē byþ forlǣten fram þām cræfte. Swā hwæðer þū sȳ, swā mæsseprēst, swā munuc, swā ċeorl, swa kempa, begā oþþe behwyrf þē sylfne on þisum, ond bēo þæt þū eart; forþām miċel hȳnð ond sceamu hyt is menn nellan wesan[36] þæt þæt hē ys ond þæt hē wesan sceal.[37]

128 [The teacher:] Ēalā, ċild, hū ēow līcaþ þeos spæċ?

129 [Pupils:] Wel hēo līcaþ ūs, ac þearle dēoplīċe sprycst ond ofer mǣþe ūre þū forþtyhst spræċe: ac sprec us æfter ūrum andgyte,[38] þæt wē magon understandan þā þingc þe þū specst.

130 [The teacher:] Iċ āhsiġe ēow, forhwī swā ġeornlīċe leorni ġē?

131 [Pupils:] Forþām wē nellaþ wesan swā stunte nȳtenu, þā nān þingc witaþ, būton gærs ond wæter.

132 [The teacher:] Ond hwæt wille ġē?

133 [Pupils:] Wyllaþ wesan wīse.

134 [The teacher:] On hwilcon wīsdōme? Wille ġē bēon prættiġe oþþe þūsenthīwe on lēasungum, lytiġe on spræcum, onglǣwlīċe, hinderġēpe, wel spreċende ond yfele þencende, swǣsum wordum underþēodde, fācn wiðinnan tȳddriende, swā swā bergyls mētton oferġeweorke,[39] wiþinnan full stenċe?

135 [Pupils:] Wē nellaþ swā wesan wīse, forþām hē nys wīs, þe mid dydrunge hyne sylfne beswicð.

136 [The teacher:] Ac hū wille ġē?

137 [Pupils:] Wē wyllaþ bēon bylewite būtan līċetunge, ond wīse þæt wē būgon fram yfele ond dōn gōda. Ġyt þēahhwæþere dēoplicor mid ūs þū smēagst, þonne yld ūre onfōn mæġe; ac sprec ūs æfter ūran ġewunon,[40] næs swā dēoplīċe.

138 [The teacher:] Ond iċ dō æal swā ġē biddaþ. Þū, cnapa, hwæt dydest tōdæġ?

139 [Pupil N:] Manega þingc iċ dyde. On þisse niht, þā þā cnyll iċ ġehȳrde, iċ ārās on mīnon bedde ond ēode tō ċyrċean, ond sang ūhtsang mid ġebrōþrum; æfter þā we sungon be eallum halgum ond dæġrēdlīċe lofsangas; æfter þysum prīm ond seofon seolmas mid lētanīan ond capitolmæssan; syþþan undertīde, ond dydon mæssan be dæġe; æfter þisum wē sungan middæġ, ond æton ond druncon ond slēpon, ond eft wē ārīson ond sungan nōn; ond nū wē synd hēr ætforan þē, ġearuwe ġehȳran hwæt þū ūs secge.

140 [The teacher:] Hwænne wylle ġē singan æfen- oþþe nihtsangc?

---

36 **menn nellan wesan:** "for a man not to want to be."

37 **wesan sceal:** "must be."

38 **æfter ūrum andgyte:** "according to our (level of) understanding."

39 **swā swā bergyls mētton oferġeweorke:** "like a tomb with a painted monument," a frequent medieval metaphor for the ostentatious and dissembling sinner.

40 **æfter ūran ġewunon:** "as we are used to."

141 [Pupil N:] Þonne hyt tīma byþ.

142 [The teacher:] Wǣre þū tōdæġ beswuncgen?

143 [Pupil N:] Iċ næs, forþām wǣrlīċe iċ mē heold.

144 [The teacher:] Ond hū þīne ġefēran?[41]

145 [Pupil N:] Hwæt mē ahsast be þām?[42] Iċ ne dear yppan þē dīgla ūre. Ānra ġehwylċ wāt ġif he beswuncgen wæs oþþe nā.

146 [The teacher:] Hwæt ytst þū on dæġ?[43]

147 [Pupil N:] Ġyt flǣscmettum iċ brūce, forðām ċild iċ eom under ġyrda drohtniende.[44]

148 [The teacher:] Hwæt māre ytst þū?

149 [Pupil N:] Wyrta ond æigra, fisc ond ċȳse, buteran ond bēana ond ealle clǣne þingc iċ ete mid miċelre þancunge.

150 [The teacher:] Swīþe waxġeorn eart þū þonne þu ealle þingc etst þe þē tōforan synd.

151 [Pupil N:] Iċ ne eom swā micel swelġere þæt iċ ealle cynn metta on ānre ġereordinge etan mæġe.

152 [The teacher:] Ac hū?

153 [Pupil N:] Iċ brūce hwīlon þisum mettum, ōþrum mid sȳfernysse, swā swā dafnað munuce, næs mid oferhropse, forþām iċ eom nān glūto.

154 [The teacher:] Ond hwæt drincst þū?

155 [Pupil N:] Ealu, ġif iċ hæbbe, oþþe wæter ġif iċ næbbe ealu.

156 [The teacher:] Ne drincst þū wīn?

157 [Pupil N:] Iċ ne eom swā spēdiġ þæt iċ mæġe bicgean mē wīn; ond wīn nys drenc ċilda ne dysgra, ac ealdra ond wīsra.

158 [The teacher:] Hwǣr slǣpst?

159 [Pupil N:] On slǣpern mid ġebrōþrum.

160 [The teacher:] Hwā āwecþ þē to ūhtsancge?

161 [Pupil N:] Hwīlon iċ ġehȳre cnyll ond iċ ārīse; hwīlon lārēow mīn āwecþ mē stīþlīċe mid gyrde.

162 [The teacher:] Ēalā, ġē ċildra ond wynsume leorneras, ēow manaþ ēower lārēow þæt ġē hȳrsumian godcundum lārum ond þæt ġē healdan ēow sylfe ǣnlīċe on ǣlcere stōwe. Gāþ þēawlīċe þonne ġē ġehȳran ċyrċean bellan, ond gāþ intō ċyrċean, ond ābūgaþ ēadmōdlīċe to halgum wēfodum, ond standaþ þēawlīċe, ond singað ānmōdlīċe, ond ġebiddaþ for ēowrum synnum, ond gāþ ūt būtan hyġelēaste tō claustre oþþe leorninga.

---

41 **hū þīne ġefēran:** "what about your companions."

42 **Hwæt ... þām:** "Why do you ask me about them."

43 **on dæġ:** not "today," but "in a day."

44 Meat-eating was forbidden by the monastic rule but allowed to the very young, who were also subject to punishment by beating.

Ælfric's *Colloquy*: Glossary

Entries are in alphabetical order except that the *ge-* prefix is ignored for alphabetization. The letters thorn (Þ/þ) and eth (Ð/ð) are alphabetized following letter *t*; letter ash (Æ/æ) is alphabetized as if it were the sequence AE (ae). Headwords of entries for verbs are the infinitive form unless otherwise indicated; headwords for nouns are nominative singular unless otherwise indicated. Accusative singular forms of nouns are identical to the nominative singular form unless otherwise noted. All other inflected forms of nouns and pronouns appear in alphabetical order within the entry and are identified as to case and number.

Abbreviations used in this glossary:

acc = accusative

adj = adjective

adv = adverb

anom = anomalous

compar = comparative

conj = conjunction

correl = correlative

dat = dative

dem = demonstrative

fem = feminine

gen = genitive

imper = imperative

impers = impersonal

indef = indefinite

indic = indicative

infin = infinitive

inflect infin = inflected infinitive

inst = instrumental

interj = interjection

interrog = interrogative

masc = masculine

neut = neuter

nom = nominative

past part = past participle

pers = person

pers = personal

pl = plural

poss = possessive

prep = preposition

pres = present tense

pres part = present participle

pret = preterite (past) tense

pron = pronoun

prop = proper

rel = relative

sing = singular

str = strong

subj = subjunctive

superl = superlative

wk = weak

ābūgan *str verb*: to bow
  ābūgaþ *imper pl* (162)
ac *conj*: but (5, 7, etc.)
ācennan *wk verb*: to produce
  ācennede *past part*: produced (96)
ādrēogan *str verb*: to endure (109)
ādrīfan *str verb*: to drive
  ādrīfaþ, ādrȳfaþ *pl pres indic* (112, 114)
æal swā: see eall
æcer *masc noun*: acre (11)
ǣfensangc *masc noun*: vespers (140)
æfter *prep with dat or acc*: according to, after (129, 137, 139)
  æfter þā: after these (139)
æig *neut noun*: egg
  æigra *acc pl* (149)
ǣl *masc noun*: eel
  ǣlas *acc pl* (65)
æl *masc noun*: awl (123)
ǣlċ *adj*: each (108, 110)
  ǣlċe *dat sing masc* (7, 11)
  ǣlċere *dat sing fem* (162)
ǣlepūta *fem noun*: "eelpout": burbot or blenny (elongated freshwater fish)
  ǣlepūtan *acc pl*: burbots, blennies (65)
ǣmtiġ *adj*: empty (110)
ǣniġ *adj*: any (18, 24)
  ǣniġne *masc acc sing* (12, 117)
  ǣniġon *dat sing* (111)
ǣnlīċe *adv*: decorously (162)
ǣnne: see ān
ǣr *neut noun*: brass; *acc sing* (98)
ǣrnemerġen *masc noun*: early morning; dawn (21)
æt *prep with dat*: at (11)
ætberstan *str verb*: to escape
  ætberstende *1st pers sing pres indic* (96)
  ætberstaþ *pl pres indic* (76)
ætforan *prep with dat*: before, in front of, in the prescence of (139)
æton: see etan
ætwesan *anom verb*: to be present
  ætwese *1st pers sing pres indic* (108)

ætwindan *str verb*: to escape (89)
āfandian *wk verb*: to prove
> **āfandod** *past part*: proven (115)

āfēdan *str verb*: to feed
> **āfēde** *1st pers sing pres subj* (100)
> **āfēst** *2nd pers sing pres indic* (87)

āġēnlǣdan *wk verb*: to lead back
> **āġēnlǣde** *1st pers sing pres indic* (19)

ahsian, axian *wk verb*: to ask
> **ahsast** *2nd pers sing pres indic* (145)
> **ahsie, ahsiġe, axie** *1st pers sing pres indic* (6, 115, 130)

ān *adj, pron*: one, only (75, 92, 126)
> **ǣnne** *acc sing masc*: a (25, 41, 84, 85)
> **ānra ġehwylċ**: each one (127, 145)
> **ānre** *dat sing fem* (151)
> **ānum** *dat sing*: one, a single (75)

ancgil, ancgel *masc noun*: hook (57, 123)
andgyte *neut noun*: understanding
> **andgyte** *dat sing* (129)

ānmōdlīċe *adv*: together, with one accord (162)
ġeanwyrde *adj*: professed
> **ġeanwyrde monuc** a monk who has taken his monastic vows (11)

ārīsan *str verb*: to arise
> **ārās** *1st pers sing pret indic* (139)
> **ārīse** *1st pers sing pres indic* (161)
> **ārīson** *pl pret indic* (139)

ārsmiþ *masc noun*: brass- or coppersmith (116)
āstigian *str verb*: to proceed, ascend
> **āstigie, āstige** *1st pers sing pres indic*: to board (a ship) (57, 96)

āweccan *wk verb*: to awaken
> **āwecþ** *3rd pers sing pres indic* (160, 161)

axie, axian: see **ahsian**

bār *masc noun*: (wild) boar (37, 41, 43, 44)
bæcere *masc noun*: baker (109)
> **bæceras** *nom pl* (11)

be *prep with dat*: by, about, with, for (49, 139, 145)

bēah *masc noun*: (finger- or arm-) ring (51)

bēan *fem noun*: bean

    bēana *acc pl* (149)

bēatan *str verb*: to beat

    bēatendra *pres part gen pl* (124)

becuman *str verb*: to come

    becuman *pl pres indic* (31)

bedd *neut noun*: bed

    bedde *dat sing* (139)

bedrīfan *str verb*: to drive

    . bedrīfon *pl pret indic* (45)

begān *str verb*: to go about

    begā *imper sing* (127)

    begæst *2nd pers sing pres indic* (10, 30)

begangan *str verb*: to go about, pursue

    began(c)ge *1st/3rd pers sing pres subj* (51, 127)

begrȳnian *wk verb*: to trap, ensnare

    begrȳnodo *past part neut pl* (31)

beġytan *str verb*: to get, acquire

    beġyst *2nd pers sing pres indic* (54)

    beġytaþ *pl pres indic* (76)

    beġyte *1st pers sing pres subj* (100)

behēfe *adj*: useful (3, 94, 102)

behwyrfan *wk verb*: to instruct, exercise

    behwyrf *imper sing* (127)

belle *wk fem noun*: bell

    bellan *acc pl* (162)

bēod *masc noun*: table (110)

bēon, wesan *anom verb*: to be (4, 5, 31, 47, 118, 119, 127, 131, 133, 134, 135, 137)

    bēo *3rd pers sing pres subj* (106), *pl pres indic preposed* (114), *imper sing* (127)

    bēoþ *pl pres indic* (58, 96, 120)

    bī *2nd pers sing pres subj* (5)

    byþ, biþ *3rd pers sing pres indic* (110, 114, 127, 141)

    eart *2nd pers sing pres indic* (127, 150)

    eom *1st pers sing pres indic* (7, 19, 27, 49, 53, 94, 147, 151, 153, 157)

    is *3rd pers sing pres indic* (10, 17, 22, 23, 39, 101, 120, 127)

nǣs *1st pers sing pret indic* (wǣs) combined with negative particle
    ne: was not (39, 143)

neom *1st pers sing pres indic* (eom) combined with negative particle
    ne: am not (17)

nys, nis *3rd pers sing pres indic* (is) combined with negative particle
    ne: is not (11, 123, 135, 157)

sy *2nd, 3rd pers sing pres subj* (3, 127)

synt, synd, syndon *pl pres indic* (1, 9, 113, 115, 139, 150)

wǣre *2nd pers sing pret indic* (38, 44, 46, 142)

wǣs *1st pers sing pret indic* (39, 145)

ys *3rd pers sing pres indic* (13, 16, 67, 73, 75, 113)

ġebeorhliċ *adj*: safe

    ġebeorhliċre *compar* (73)

beran *str verb*: to carry (15)

bergyls *masc noun*: tomb, sepulchre (134)

besenċean *str verb*: to sink (75)

beswican *str verb*: to ensnare, deceive

    beswiċe *1st pers sing pres indic* (79)

    beswicst *2nd pers sing pres indic* (78)

    beswicþ *3rd pers sing pres indic* (135)

beswincgan *str verb*: to beat, flog

    beswungen, beswuncgen *past part* (4, 5, 142, 145)

betǣċan *wk verb*: to entrust, deliver; hunt

    betǣċe *1st pers sing pres indic* (21, 35)

betwenan *adv*: in between (7)

betweoh, betwux *prep with dat*: among (119, 120, 121, 127)

beþurfan *anom verb with gen*: to need

    beþurfon *pl pres indic* (111)

bicgean *wk verb:* to buy (157)

    bicge *1st pers sing pres indic* (96, 104)

    ġebicge *1st pers sing pres indic* (100)

    biġþ *3rd pers sing pres indic* (62)

    ġebohtest *3rd pers sing pret indic*: got, acquired (99)

biddan *str verb*: to ask, request

    biddaþ *pl pres indic* (1, 138)

    ġebiddaþ *imper pl* (162)

biġġenceare *masc noun*: worker

    biġġenceras *acc pl* (116)

biġleofa *masc noun*: livelihood, sustinence

    biġleofan *acc sing* (55, 127)

biġþ: see bicgean

bilewit, bylewit *adj*: mild

    bilewitne *acc sing masc* (5)

    bylewite *nom pl masc* (137)

binn *fem noun*: bin, manger

    binne *acc sing* (15)

blāwan *str verb*: to blow

    blāwendra *pres part* (124)

bliss *fem noun*: happiness, satisfaction

    blisse *dat sing* (106)

ġebohtest: see bicgean

brǣdan *str verb*: to roast, broil (113)

    tō brǣdenne *inflect infin* (113)

brēdan *str verb*: to weave

    brēde *1st pers sing pres indic* (31)

bridd *masc noun*: young bird

    briddas *acc pl* (88)

brīdelþwancg *masc noun*: rein

    brīdelþwancgas *acc pl* (104)

broþ *neut noun*: broth (112)

ġebrōþor *anom noun*: brother

    ġebrōþrum *dat pl*: the brothers (i.e., the speaker's fellow monks) (7, 139, 159)

brūcan *wk verb with dat*: to enjoy, to make use of

    brūcaþ *3rd pers pl pres indic* (108)

    brūce *1st pers sing pres indic* (147, 153)

    brȳcð *3rd pers sing pres indic* (106)

būgan *str verb*: to depart

    būgon *pl pret indic* (137)

būtan/būton *prep with dat, conj*: except, provided that, unless, without (3, 5, 32, 33, 83, 104, 106, 108, 109, 110, 112, 114, 118, 123, 124, 131, 137, 162)

butere *fem noun*: butter (19)

    buteran *acc sing* (149)

buterġeþwēor *neut noun*: freshly churned butter-mass (108)

buteric *masc noun*: leather bottle

    butericas *acc pl* (104)

bylewit, bylewite: see bilewit

bylig *masc noun*: bellows
      byliga *gen pl* (124)
bysgod on: busy with (7)

cann, canst: see **cunnan**
capitolmæsse *fem noun*: capitular mass
      capitolmæssan *dat sing* (139)
ċeaster *fem noun*: city/town
      ċeastre *dat sing* (61)
ċeasterwara *fem pl noun*: city people, city dwellers (63)
ċeorl *masc noun*: freeman, peasant (127)
ċild *neut noun*: child (147); children (128)
      ċild(r)a *nom pl* (1, 162); *gen pl* (157)
clǣne *adj*: clean (59, 149)
clauster *neut noun*: cloister
      claustre *dat sing* (162)
cleafa *masc noun*: cellar
      cleafan *acc sing* (108)
cnapa *masc noun*: boy, servant (138)
      cnapan *acc sing* (13)
cnyll *masc noun*: sound of a bell, knell (139, 161)
crabba *masc noun*: crab
      crabban *acc pl*: crabs (69)
cræft *masc noun*: craft, skill, occupation (25, 30, 51, 52, 102, 106, 109, 111, 119, 127)
      cræfta *gen pl* (116)
      cræftas *acc pl* (120)
      cræfte *dat sing* (54, 104, 105, 108, 110, 111, 112, 123, 125, 127)
      cræftes *gen sing* (113)
culter *masc noun*: coulter, a detachable iron blade for a plow which made the vertical cut in the soil (123)
      cultre *dat sing* (11)
      ġefæstnodon ... cultre with the coulter attached (11)
cunnan *pret pres verb*: to know; know how to (5)
      cann *1st pers sing pres* (25, 83, 92)
      canst *2nd pers sing pres* (24, 32, 52, 82)
      cunnon *pl pres indic* (8)
      cūþe *1st pers sing pret subj* (83)

cwic *adj*: alive (96)

ġecwylman *wk verb*: destroy, kill (75)

cyld *neut noun*: chill, cold

　　　cylde *dat sing* (13)

cyle *masc noun*: cold (19)

cyning *masc noun*: king

　　　cyncges *gen sing* (29)

　　　cyngce *dat sing* (49, 94)

cynn *neut noun*: kind, sort (151)

　　　cynnes *gen sing* (104)

ċȳpan *wk verb*: to sell (100)

　　　ċȳpe *1st pers sing pres indic* (96)

　　　ċȳpst *2nd pers sing pres indic* (60)

cȳpmann *masc noun*: merchant

　　　cȳpmenn *nom pl* (11)

ċyriċe *fem noun*: church

　　　ċyrċean *dat/gen sing* (139, 162)

ċȳse *masc noun*: cheese (19, 149)

cȳsgerunn *neut noun*: cheese-curd (108)

dæġ *masc noun*: day (7, 11, 14, 19, 146)

　　　dæġe *dat sing* (139)

dæġrǣd *neut noun*: dawn (11)

dæġrēdlīċe *adj*: appropriate for dawn or morning (139)

dǣl *masc noun*: region

　　　sǣlīċe dǣlas the high seas (96)

dafnian *wk verb*: to beseem, befit

　　　dafnað *3rd pers sing pres indic* (153)

dear: see **durran**

dēoplīċe *adv*: deeply, profoundly (129, 137)

　　　dēoplicor *compar* (137)

ġedeorf *neut noun*: work, labour (16, 17, 18, 100)

deorfan *str verb*: to work, labour (92)

　　　(ġe)deorfe *1st pers sing pres indic* (11, 21)

dēoror *adv compar*: at a higher price (100)

dēorwyrþe *adj*: precious, valuable (98)

　　　dȳrwyrþe *acc pl neut* (96)

dēst: see **dōn**

digol *neut noun*: secret

　　　digla *acc pl* (145)

dōn *str verb*: to do, make (114, 126, 137)

  dēst *2nd pers sing pres indic* (14, 48)

  dō *1st pers sing pres indic* (15, 19, 67, 138)

  dōþ *pl pres indic* (91)

  dyde *1st pers sing pret indic* (139)

  dydest *2nd pers sing pret indic* (138)

  dydon *pl pret indic* (139)

drenc *masc noun*: drink (124, 157)

drīfan *str verb*: to drive

  drīfe *1st pers sing pres indic* (19)

drincan *str verb*: to drink

  drincst *2nd pers sing pres indic* (154, 156)

  druncon *pl pret indic* (139)

drohtnian *wk verb*: to conduct oneself, behave, live

  drohtniende *pres part* (147)

druncon: see **drincan**

durran *pret pres verb*: to dare, presume

  dear *1st pers sing pres indic* (145)

  durre *1st pers sing pres subj* (11)

dyde, dydest, dydon: see **dōn**

dydrunge *fem noun*: delusion; *dat sing* (135)

dyrstiġ *adj*: daring, brave (44)

dȳrwyrþe: see **dēorwyrþe**

dysiġ *adj*: dizzy, foolish

  dysgra *as noun gen pl*: of foolish ones (157)

ēa *fem noun*: river; *dat sing* (57, 73)

ēac *adv*: also (9, 13, 75, 92)

ēadmōdlīċe *adv*: humbly, reverently (162)

ēalā *interj*: oh, hey, well (an attention-getting word without lexical content)
  (1, 11, 20, 21, 115, 126, 127, 128, 162)

ealdordōm *masc noun*: pre-eminence (121)

ealdormann *masc noun*: nobleman

  ealdormannum *dat pl* (94)

ealdorscype *masc noun*: supremacy, sovereignty (120)

ealdra *adj, as noun, gen pl*: of old ones (157)

eall(e) *adj*: all (21, 114, 120, 122, 149, 150, 151)

  eallum *dat pl* (94, 106, 124, 125, 127, 139)

  ealra *gen pl* (96)

  eal swā, æal swā just as (99, 138)

ealu *neut noun*: ale (155)

efne *interj*: indeed (108, 115)

eft *adv*: again, thereafter, afterwards (21, 92, 139)

eġe *masc noun*: fear

        eġe *dat sing* (11)

ēhtan *wk verb*: to pursue, chase

        ēhton *3rd pers pl pres indic* (31)

ele *masc noun*: oil (98)

ēode: see **gān**

eorþtilþ *fem noun*: agriculture (122)

ēow, ēower, ēowre, ēowrum: see **ġē**

erian *wk verb*: to plow (11)

etan *str verb*: to eat (151)

            etaþ *3rd pers pl pres indic* (90, 112, 114)

            ete *1st pers sing pres indic* (149)

            æton *pl pret indic* (139)

            ytst, etst *2nd pers sing pres indic* (146, 148, 150)

fācn *neut noun*: deceit, guile (134)

fæc *neut noun*: a portion of time (110)

fǣrlīċe *adv*: suddenly, rapidly (45)

fæstnian *wk verb*: to fasten

        ġefæstnodon *past part as adj*: fastened (11)

fæt *neut noun*: vessel, utensil

        fata *gen pl* (125)

fǣtels *masc noun*: pouch, bag

        fǣtelsas *acc pl* (104)

fǣtt *adj*: rich (112)

fagc *fem noun*: plaice (a red and brown European flounder); *acc pl* (69)

faran *str verb*: to go (73)

fēdan *str verb*: to feed (90)

        fēdaþ *pl pres indic* (91)

        fētt *3rd pers sing pres indic* (51, 122)

(ġe)fēhst: see **fōn**

fela/feala *pron*: many, much (69, 79, 98)

        swā fela ... swā as many ... as (63)

feld *masc/neut noun*: field

        felda *dat sing* (11)

fell *neut noun*: skin; *acc pl* (104)

ġefēncge, ġefēo: see **fōn**

feoh *neut noun*: money (55)

ġefēra *masc noun*: companion

> **ġefēran** *nom pl* (8); *acc sing* (12); *nom/acc pl* (75, 115, 127, 144)
>
> **ġefērum** *dat pl* (22)

ġefērscype *masc noun*: fellowship, society (112)

fētt: see **fēdan**

fisc *masc noun*: fish (149); *acc sing* (75)

> **fixas** *acc pl* (56, 58, 60)

fiscere *masc noun*: fisherman (53, 123)

> **fisceras** *nom pl* (9)

fixas: see **fisc**

fixian *wk verb*: to fish

> **fixast** *2nd pers sing pres* (66)

flǣscmete *masc noun*: meat

> **flǣscmettas** *acc pl* (112)
>
> **flǣscmettum** *dat pl* (147)

flaxe *fem noun*: flask, leather bottle

> **flaxan** *acc pl* (104)

ġeflit *neut noun*: dispute

> **ġeflitu** *acc pl* (127)

floc *neut noun*: flat fish, flounder; *acc pl* (69)

foddor *neut noun*: fodder (127)

folc *neut noun*: people

> **follce** *dat sing* (94)

ġefōn *str verb*: to catch (63, 73, 92)

> **fēhst** *2nd pers sing pres* (68)
>
> **ġefēhst** *2nd pers sing pres indic* (36, 56, 64, 75)
>
> **ġefēncge** *1st/2nd pers sing pret indic* (42, 43)
>
> **ġefēo, ġefō** *1st pers sing pres indic* (37, 49)
>
> **ġefōþ** *3rd pers pres pl* (76)

for *prep with dat*: on account of, because of (5, 11, 13, 21, 77)

forbīġean *wk verb*: to despise, to shun (110)

forewerd *adj*: early

> **forewerdne** *acc sing masc* (19)

forhtfull *adj*: timid, frightened (47)

forhwī *interr adv* why (66, 72, 74, 89, 126, 130)
forlǣtan *str verb*: to neglect, forsake
    forlǣst *2nd pers sing pres indic* (89)
    forlǣt *3rd pers sing pres indic* (127)
    forlǣten *past part*: forsaken (127)
forlidenes *fem noun*: shipwreck
    forlidenesse *acc sing* (96)
forswelgan *str verb*: to swallow up
    forswelġen *3rd pers pl pres subj* (19)
forþām *conj*: because (1, 17, 39, 47, 49, 67, 73, 75, 90, 92, 113, 122, 124, 127,
    131, 135, 143, 147, 153)
    forþām þe *conj*: because (90)
forþtihan *str verb*: to draw forth
    forþtyhst *2nd pers sing pres indic* (129)
    forþtihan sprǣċe speak (129)
forþȳ *conj*: therefore (114)
fracod *adj*: evil, worthless (3)
fram *prep with dat*: from, by (5, 89, 112, 114, 127, 137)
    framiġe *3rd pers sing pres subj* (127)
frēċnys *fem noun*: peril, danger
    frēċnysse *acc sing* (76)
framian *wk verb*: to benefit
fremman *wk verb*: to help, benefit
    fremaþ *3rd pers sing pres indic* (105, 106, 109)
    fremode *3rd pers sing pret subj* (100)
frēoh *adj*: free (17)
fugel *masc noun*: bird
    fugelas *acc pl*: birds (78, 79)
fuglere *masc noun*: fowler (78)
    fugleras *nom pl* (4)
ful *adj*: full, complete
    fulne *masc acc sing* (11)
full *adj*: foul (134)
furþon *adv*: even (110, 112, 126)
    ne furþon þæt ān *adv phrase*: not even (108)
furþra *adj compar*: greater, superior (119)
fyllan *wk verb*: to fill, feed (15)
    ġefylde *past part* (21)
    ġefylð *3rd pers sing pres indic* (108)

fyrmest *adv*: first (120)
fȳrspearca *masc noun*: fiery spark
      fȳrspearcan *acc pl* (124)

gād *fem noun*: cattle goad
      gāde *acc sing* (123)
ġegaderungc *fem noun*: community (118)
gādīsen *neut noun*: (iron-tipped) cattle goad
      gādīsene *dat sing* (13)
gærs *neut noun*: grass (131)
gān *anom verb*: to go
      ēode *1st pers sing pret indic* (139)
      gā *1st pers sing pres indic* (11)
      gāþ *imper pl* (162)
ġe *conj*: and, also
      ġe ... ġe: both ... and (19)
      ġe ... ond: both ... and (94)
ġē *pers pron*: you (pl) (2, 4, 110, 112, 114, 130, 132, 134, 136, 138, 140, 162)
      ēow *dat pl* (96, 102, 106, 108, 120, 125, 128, 130, 162)
      ēower *gen* (104, 106, 114, 125, 162)
      ēowre *poss adj acc pl* (112)
      ēowrum *poss adj dat sing/dat pl* (108, 112, 162)
ġēa *interj*: yea, yes (17, 19, 23, 33, 83, 92)
ġearkian *wk verb*: to prepare
      ġearkie *1st pers sing pres indic* (104)
ġearu *adj*: ready
      ġearuwe *nom/acc pl* (91, 139)
ġeornlīċe *adv*: diligently (127, 130)
ġif/ġyf *conj*: if (58, 85, 112, 114, 145, 155)
gistliþe *adj*: hospitable (106)
glæs *neut noun*: glass (98)
gluto *masc noun*: glutton (153)
God *masc noun*: God
      Godes *gen sing* (120)
gōd *neut noun*: good thing
      gōda *acc pl* (137)
godcundum *adj dat pl*: sacred, divine (162)

gōde *adj*: good (115, 127)
godspell *neut noun*: gospel
    godspelle *dat sing* (120)
gold *masc noun*: gold (98)
goldsmiþ, golsmiþ *masc noun*: goldsmith (116, 126)
grene *adj*: green, i.e., raw (112)
grīn *neut noun*: snare
    grīnum *dat pl* (79)
ġyf: see **ġif**
ġymm *masc noun* jewel
    ġymmas *acc pl*: jewels (98)
ġyrd *fem noun*: rod, stick
    ġyrda *dat sing* (147)
    ġyrde *dat sing* (161)
ġyrstandæġ *masc noun*: yesterday (39)
ġyt *adv*: yet, still (137, 147)

habban *wk verb*: to have (85, 91, 115)
    habbaþ *pl pres indic* (127)
    hæbbe *1st pers sing pres indic* (13, 19, 81, 115, 118, 155)
    hæfst *2nd pers sing pres indic* (6, 12, 18, 80, 117)
    hæfþ *3rd pers sing pres indic* (123)
    næbbe *1st pers sing pres* ne + hæbbe: do not have (155)
hacod *masc noun*: pike/mullet
    hacodas *acc pl* (65)
hæbbe, hæfst, hæfþ: see **habban**
ġehæftan *wk verb*: catch
    ġehæftað *pl pres* (57)
hælfter *fem noun*: halter
    hælftra *acc pl* (104)
ġehæp *adj*: suitable, convenient
    ġehæppre *fem dat sing* (31)
hærfæst *masc noun*: harvest
    hærfæste *dat sing* (88)
hǣrincg *masc noun*: herring
    hǣrincgas *acc pl* (69)
hǣtu *fem noun*: heat
    hǣte *dat sing* (19)

hafoc *masc noun*: hawk (80, 84, 85)
    hafocas *acc pl* (87)
    hafoce *dat sing* (79)
haliġ *adj*: holy (as noun: saint)
    halgum *dat pl* (139, 162)
hām *masc noun*: home; *dat sing* (11)
hara *masc noun*: hare
    haran *acc pl* (37)
hās *adj*: hoarse (13)
hē *pers pron*: he, it (23, 50, 51, 75, 113, 127, 135, 145)
    hine *acc sing* (45, 135)
    his *gen sing* (49, 113, 120, 127)
healdan, heoldan *str verb*: to hold (120, 121, 162)
    heold *1st pers sing pret* (143)
hēddern *neut noun*: storeroom, storehouse
    hēdderna *acc pl* (108)
hēo *pers pron fem*: it (129)
heold, heoldan: see **healdan**
heora: see **hīġ**
heort *masc noun*: hart, adult male red deer (37)
    heortas *acc pl* (41, 43)
heorte *fem noun*: heart
    heortan *acc sing* (110)
hēr *adv*: here (99, 100, 139)
hider *adv*: here (96)
hīġ, hī *pers pron nom/acc pl*: they, them (11, 15, 19, 21, 31, 42, 57, 62, 82,
        83, 88, 90, 91, 92, 100, 104)
    heora *gen pl* (15, 19, 100)
    him *dat pl* (104)
hīġ *neut noun*: hay (15)
hīġ *interj*: a cry of distress or sympathy (16)
hīġdifæt *neut noun*: leather-bottle
    hīġdifætu *acc pl* (104)
him: see **hīġ**
hinderġēpe *adj*: wily, deceitful (134)
hine, his: see **hē**
hit, hyt *pers pron*: it (3, 5, 11, 16, 17, 58, 73, 96, 120, 123, 141)

hlæst *neut noun*: load, cargo, freight
    hlæstum *dat pl* (96)
hlāf *masc noun*: loaf (of bread) (124)
    hlāfe *dat sing* (110)
hlāford *masc noun*: lord (11, 114); *acc sing* (21)
    hlāforde *dat sing* (19)
    hlāfordes *gen sing* (11)
hors *neut noun*: horse (51)
    horsum *dat pl* (127)
hran *masc noun*: whale
    hranes *gen sing* (73)
hrēam *masc noun*: noise (yelling)
    hrēame *dat sing* (13)
hreawe *adj*: raw, uncooked (112)
hū *interrog adv*: how, what about (10, 30, 34, 42, 44, 56, 78, 87, 95, 103,
    107, 128, 136, 144, 152)
hund *masc noun*: dog (85)
    hundas *nom/acc pl* (31, 45)
    hundum *dat pl* (19, 35)
hunta *masc noun*: hunter (27, 47, 49)
    huntan *nom pl* (9)
huntian *wk verb*: to hunt (32, 33)
huntnoþ *masc noun*: hunting, the hunt
    huntnoþe *dat sing* (38)
huntung *fem noun*: the hunt; the catch, the product of the hunt
    huntunge *dat sing* (39, 48, 73)
hūs *neut noun*: house; *acc pl* (125)
hwā *interrog and indef pronoun*: who?, what?, someone, something (62, 108,
    115, 160)
hwæl *masc noun*: whale (70, 73)
    hwælas *acc pl* (76)
hwænne *adv*: when? (140)
hwǣr *adv*: where? (60, 158)
hwæs *interrog pron gen sing*: whose? (28)
hwæt *interrog pron*: what? (3, 6, etc.)

hwæþer *conj*: (marks a question)
    hwæþer we ... magon? can we? (109)
    hwæþer we beþurfon? do we need? (111)
hwæþer þe *conj*: or (85)
hwætlíce *adv*: quickly
    hwætlícor *compar*: as quickly as possible (127)
hwām *interrog pron dat sing*: (to) whom (109)
hwanon *adv*: (from) whence (123)
hwīl *fem noun*: time
    hwīlum, hwīlon *dat pl as adv*: sometimes (37, 51, 67, 79, 96, 153,
      161)
hwilċ *interr pron, adj*: which, what kind of (108, 119, 121, 125)
    hwilċe *acc pl* (36, 64, 97)
    hwilċne, hwylċne *acc sing masc* (26, 52, 85)
    hwilċon *dat sing masc* (134)
hwīlum, hwīlon: see **hwīl**
hwistlung *fem noun*: whistling
    hwistlunge *dat sing* (79)
ġehwyrfan *wk verb*: to turn
    ġehwyrfed *past part* (110)
hȳd *fem noun*: hide (i.e., skin of an animal)
    hȳda *acc pl* (104)
hyġelēast *fem noun*: thoughtless behaviour; jesting, buffoonery
    hyġelēaste *dat sing* (162)
hynð *fem noun*: humiliation, shame (127)
ġehȳran *wk verb*: to hear (139)
    ġehȳran *pl pres indic* (162)
    ġehȳrde *1st pers sing pret indic* (139)
    ġehȳre *1st pers sing pres indic* (161)
hyrde *masc noun*: custody, keeping (108)
hȳrsumian *wk verb*: to be obedient to (162)
hyt: see **hit**

iċ *pers pron*: I (6, etc.)
    mē: *dat/acc* (31, etc.)
īdel *adj*: idle (3)
intō *prep with dat*: into (162)
īsene *adj*: iron (116)
    īsenne *acc pl* (124)

iugian, iucian *wk verb*: to join, yoke
> **iugie** *1st pers sing pres indic* (11)
> **ġeiukodan** *past part as adj* (11)

kempa *masc noun*: warrior (127)

ġelæċċan *wk verb*: to catch
> **ġelæhtest** *2nd pers sing pret indic* (40)

ġelǣdan *wk verb*: to bring
> **lǣde** *1st pers sing pres indic* (21)
> **ġelǣdst** *2nd pers sing pres indic* (97)

ġelæhtest: see *ġelæċċan*

lǣs *fem noun*: pasture
> **lǣse** *dat sing* (19, 21)

lǣs *compar adj*: smaller
> **lǣssan** *acc sing masc* (85)

lǣtan *str verb*: to let, allow
> **lǣte** *1st pers sing pres* (88)

lamprede *fem noun*: lamprey
> **lampredan** *acc pl* (65)

lancge *adv*: long (110)

land *neut noun*: land, country
> **lande** *dat sing* (96)

lār *fem noun*: learning, teaching
> **lāre** *dat sing* (5)
> **lārum** *dat pl* (162)

lārēow *masc noun*: teacher, master (1, 161, 162)

lēasung *fem noun*: deceit, artifice, lying
> **lēasungum** *dat pl* (134)

leax *masc noun*: salmon
> **leaxas** *acc pl* (69)

lēden *neut noun or adj*: Latin (7)

lencgten *masc noun*: spring; *dat sing* (88)

lēof *adj*: dear (11); *as a noun*: (dear) Sir (17, 19)
> **lēofre** *compar*: preferable (5, 75, 124)
> **lēofre is mē** I would rather (75)
> **ūs lēofre is/lēofre ys ūs** we would rather (5, 124)

leornere *masc noun*: scholar, pupil
       leorneras *nom pl* (162)
leornian *wk verb*: to learn (7)
       leornie *pl pres indic preposed* (130)
leorning, leornung *fem noun*: learning, study
       leorninga, leornunge *dat sing* (4, 162)
lētanīa *masc noun*: litany
       lētanīan *dat sing* (139)
leþerhosu *fem noun*: leather gaiter or legging
       leþerhosa *acc pl* (104)
līcaþ: see **līcian**
līċetunge *fem noun dat sing*: deceit, hypocrisy (137)
līcian *wk impers verb*: to please
       līcaþ *3rd pers sing pres indic* (128, 129)
līf *neut noun*: life (109)
līm *masc noun*: bird-lime (a sticky material that is spread on branches
       to trap little birds)
       līme *dat sing* (79)
litlincg *masc noun*: child
       litlincgas *nom sing* (110)
loc *neut noun*: fold
       loca *acc pl* (19)
lofsangas *masc pl noun*: Lauds ("songs of praise") (139)
lopystre *fem noun*: lobster
       lopystran *acc pl* (69)
losian *wk verb*: to be lost, perish, go bad
       losaþ *3rd pers sing pres indic* (108)
lustlīċe *adv*: willingly (85)
       lustlicor *compar* (51)
lutian *wk verb*: to hide, lurk (11)
lyre *masc noun*: loss; *dat sing* (96)
lytiġe *adj*: crafty (134)

mæġ, mæġe: see **magan**
mægen *neut noun*: strength, power (110)
mæsseprēst *masc noun*: priest (127)
mæsse *fem noun*: mass
      mæssan *acc sing* (139)

mæstlingc *neut noun*: brass (98)

mǣþ *fem noun*: measure, ability

    mǣþe *dat sing* (129)

magan *str verb*: can; to be able, be competent

    mæġ *1st pers sing pre indic* (33, 63, 75)

    mæġe *1st pers sing pres subj* (137, 151, 157)

    magon *pl pres indic* (109, 110, 112, 113, 129)

    miht *2nd pers sing pres indic* (126)

mancgere *masc noun*: merchant, trader (93)

maneġ, maniġ *adj*: many

    manegum *dat pl* (73)

    manega *acc pl* (139)

    maneġra *gen pl* (116)

    mæniġe/maniġe *nom pl* (76, 91); *acc pl* (92)

manian *wk verb*: to remind, exhort

    manaþ *3rd pers sing pres indic* (162)

manna, mannes: see **mon**

māra *compar adj*: more

māran *acc sing masc*: greater, larger (85, 86)

    māre *acc pl* (11); *acc sing neut* (14, 15, 148)

max *neut noun*: net; *acc pl* (31); *acc sing* (57)

    maxum *dat pl* (31)

melkan *str verb*: to milk

    melke *1st pers sing pres indic* (19)

menn: see **mon**

mereswȳn *neut noun*: dolphin, porpoise; *acc pl* (69)

metan *str verb*: to paint

    metton *past part dat sing neut* (134)

mete *masc noun*: food; *dat sing* (59, 106, 110)

    metta *gen pl* (151)

    mettum *dat pl* (108, 153)

miċel *adj/adv* much, great; *nom sing masc* (16, 17, 21, 67, 127, 151)

    miċċlan *dat sing* (96)

    miċelne *acc sing masc* (76)

    miċelre *dat sing fem* (149)

mid *prep with dat*: with (7, etc.)

middæġ *masc noun*: sext (139)

miht: see **magan**

mīn *poss adj*: my (100, 102, 106, 161)
> **mīne** *masc/neut acc pl* (19, 51, 57, 75, 96)
> **mīnes** *masc gen sing* (11); *neut gen sing* (77)
> **mīnne** *acc sing masc* (100)
> **mīnra** *gen pl* (96)
> **mȳnum, mīnum, mīnon** *dat sing* (19, 73, 96, 104, 108, 110, 112, 123, 125, 139)

mistlīċ *adj*: various plentiful
> **mistlīċe** *nom/acc pl* (47, 125)
> **mistlīċes** *gen sing* (104)
> **mistlīċra** *gen pl* (116)

mōd *neut noun*: heart, mind
> **mōdes** *gen sing* (77)

mon *masc noun*: man
> **manna** *gen pl* (108)
> **mannes** *gen sing* (110)
> **menn** *dat sing* (127)

monuc, munuc *masc noun*: monk (2, 115, 127)
> **munuce** *dat sing* (153)

morġen *masc noun*: morning (19)

munus: see **monuc**

musle *fem noun*: mussel
> **muslan** *acc pl* (69)

myne *masc noun*: minnow
> **mynas** *acc pl* (65)

mȳnum: see **mīn**

nā *adv, conj*: not, not at all (110, 123, 145)
> **nā þæt ān** *adv phrase*: not only (75)
> **nā þæt ān ænne**: not only the one (92)

næbbe: see **habban**

nǣdl *fem noun*: needle (123)

næs *adv*: not at all (3, 137, 153)

nān *pron*: none, not one (104, 106, 114, 131, 153)

ne *adv, conj*: not, nor (5, 32, 47, 96, 108, 110, 113, 114, 125, 126, 145, 151, 156, 157)

nellan *anom verb*: to be unwilling (5, 127)
> **nele** *3rd pers sing pres indic* (104)
> **nellaþ** *pl pres indic* (110, 131, 135)
> **nelle** *1st pers sing pres indic* (90, 92, 100)

nēodþearf *adj*: necessary (102, 113)

    nēodþearfe *acc pl* (115)

nett *neut noun*: net

    netum, nettum *dat pl* (31, 32, 33, 43, 79)

niċ *interj*: not me (65)

niht *fem noun*: night (21, 139)

nihtsangc *masc noun*: compline (140)

ġeniman *str verb*: to take

    ġenime/ġenyme *1st pers pres indic* (57, 59, 88)

nōn *neut noun*: nones (139)

notian *wk verb with dat*: to use, enjoy

    notaþ *3rd pers sing pres indic* (125)

nū *adv*: now (13, 139)

ġenyme: see ġeniman

nytenu *neut pl noun*: beasts, cattle (131)

nytenys *fem noun*: cowardice

    nytenyssæ *dat sing* (77)

nytwyrþnes *fem noun*: usefulness, utility

    nytwyrþnessæ *gen sing* (101)

of *prep with dat*: of, from (22, 54, 104, 124)

ofer *prep with acc or dat*: over, past, beyond (19, 91, 92, 96, 129)

oferġeweork *neut noun*: superstructure, sepulchral monument

    oferġeweorke *dat sing* (134)

oferhrops *fem noun*: voracity

    oferhropse *dat sing* (153)

oferwintran *wk verb*: to get through the winter, over-winter (104)

ofslēan *str verb*: to kill (75)

    ofslēa *1st pers sing pres indic* (31)

    ofslōh *1st pers sing pret indic* (43)

ofstikian *wk verb*: to stab (to death); kill by stabbing (44)

    ofstikode *past part* (45)

on *prep with dat or acc*: in, on, into, onto (2, etc.)

onbelæden *wk verb*: to inflict, deliver, mete out

ond *conj*: and

ondswerian *wk verb*: to answer

    ondsweraþ *3rd pers sing pres indic* (124)

ondwyrdan *str verb*: to answer

    ondwyrt *3rd pers sing pres indic* (126)

onfōn *str verb*: to take, receive (137)
onglǣwlīċe *adj*: artful (134)
ostre *fem noun*: oyster
      ostran *acc pl* (69)
ōþer *pron, adj*: other
      ōþre *acc pl* (92, 116)
      ōþron, ōþrum *dat pl* (127, 153)
oþþæt *conj*: until (31)
oþþe *conj*: or (11, 51, 75, 104, 106, 108, 109, 124, 127, 134, 140, 145, 155, 162)
oxa *masc noun*: ox
      oxan *acc pl* (11, 13, 21)
      oxan *dat pl*: ġeiukodan oxan with the oxen yoked (11)
      oxena *gen pl* (15)
oxanhyrde *masc noun*: oxherd (20)
      oxanhyrdas *nom pl* (11)

pæll *masc noun*: purple garment
      pællas *acc pl*: purple garments (98)
pinne *fem noun*: flask, bottle
      pinnan *acc pl* (104)
pliht *masc noun*: danger, risk
      plihte *dat sing* (96)
plyhtlic *adj*: dangerous (73)
prættiġe *adj*: sly, cunning (134)
prīm *neut noun*: prime (139)
pusa *masc noun*: bag, scrip
      pusan *acc pl* (104)

rā *masc noun*: male roe deer (a small European deer)
      rānn *acc pl* (37)
ġerǣdan *wk verb*: to read
      ġerǣd *3rd pers sing pres indic* (120)
ġerǣde *neut noun*: trappings
      ġerǣda *acc pl* (104)
rǣge *fem noun*: female roe deer
      rǣgan *acc pl* (37)
rānn: see rā
rēaf *neut noun*: garment; *acc pl* (98)

reċċan *wk verb with gen*: to care for
    reċċaþ *3rd pers sing pres indic* (113)
    rēċe *pl pres indic preposed* (3)
ġereord *neut noun*: voice, speech, language
    ġereorde *dat sing* (7)
ġereording *fem noun*: meal
    ġereordinge, ġererduncge *dat sing* (106, 151)
rēwyt *neut noun*: rowing, travelling (67)
rīċe *neut noun*: kingdom (120)
riht *adj*: right, proper (3)
rihtwisnes *fem noun*: righteousness
    rihtwisnesse *acc sing* (120)
rōwan *str verb*: to travel by water, sail
    rōwe *1st pers sing pres* (96)

sǣ *masc/fem noun*: sea; *dat sing* (66, 67, 68, 96)
sǣcocc *masc noun*: cockle, shellfish
    sǣcoccas *acc pl* (69)
sæġest, sæġst, sæġþ: see **secgan**
sǣliċ *adj*: of the sea, marine, maritime
    sǣliċe *acc masc pl* (96)
sang: see **singan**
sang *masc noun*: singing
    sange *dat sing* (7)
sceal: see **sculan**
sceamu *fem noun*: shame (127)
scēap *neut noun*: sheep; *acc pl* (19)
scēaphyrde *masc noun*: shepherd (18)
    scēphyrdas *nom pl* (9)
scear *masc noun*: (plow)share, a detachable iron blade for a plow which made
    a horizontal cut in the soil and turned the furrow (123)
    ġefæstnodon sceare with the plowshare attached (11)
scearn *neut noun*: manure, muck (15)
sceatt *masc noun*: money, profit
    sceat *acc sing* (76)
    sceotan *acc pl* (65)

sceōh *masc noun*: shoe
    sceōs *acc pl* (104)
sceoldon: see **sculan**
sceōs: see **sceōh**
sceota *masc noun*: trout
sceōwyrhta *masc noun*: shoemaker (101)
    sce(ō)wyrhtan *nom pl* (9); *dat sing* (123)
scēphyrdas: see **scēaphyrde**
scrūd *neut noun*: clothing (55)
scrȳdan *wk verb*: to clothe, dress
    scrȳt *3rd pers sing pres indic* (51)
sculan *str verb*: must, shall, ought to
    sceal *1st, 3rd pers sing indic pres* (11, 15, 47, 127)
    sceoldon *pl pret indic* (83)
    hwæt sceoldon hīġ mē: what use would they be to me? (83)
gescȳ *neut pl noun*: footwear (104)
scyp *neut noun*: ship/boat; *acc sing* (57, 96)
    scypa *acc pl* (125)
    scype *dat sing nom* (73)
    scypum *dat pl* (73)
se *dem pron*: the, that (118, 122, 123, 125, 126, 127)
    þā *nom/acc pl* (21, 59, 89, 91, 96, 113, 115, 129, 131)
    þǣm *dat sing masc/neut* (21, 127)
    þǣm, þām *dat pl* (31, 145)
    þæne *acc sing masc* (85, 86)
    þænne *acc sing masc* (85)
    þǣre *dat sing fem* (11)
    þæt *acc sing neut* (127)
    þone *acc sing masc* (85)
sealt *neut noun*: salt
    sealtes *gen sing* (108)
sealtere *masc noun*: salter (105)
    sealteras *nom pl* (9)
seamere *masc noun*: tailor (123)
sēċean *wk verb*: to seek
    sēċeað *imper pl* (120)
secgan *str verb*: to say
    sæġest/sæġst/seġst *2nd pers sing pres indic* (10, 77, 78, 93, 124)

secge *1st pers sing pres indic* (94); *2nd pers sing pres subj* (139)

seġð, sæġþ *3rd pers sing pres indic* (123, 125, 127)

selcūþ *adj*: rare, marvellous

selcūþe *acc pl* (98)

seldon *adv*: seldom (67)

seofon *num*: seven (7, 139)

seolm *masc noun*: psalm

seolmas *acc pl* (139)

seoloforsmiþ *masc noun*: silversmith (116)

ġesēon *str verb*: to see

ġesewen *past part* (110)

sēoþan *str verb*: to boil (113)

tō sēoþenne *inflect infin* (113)

settan *wk verb*: to set

sette *1st pers sing pres indic* (31)

sibb *fem noun*: peace, concord (127)

sīde *fem noun*: silk

sīdan *acc pl* (98)

singan *wk verb*: to sing (140)

sang *1st pers sing pret indic* (139)

sincge *1st sing pres indic* (7)

singaþ *imper pl* (162)

sungon *2nd pers pl pret indic* (139)

slǣpan *str verb*: to sleep

slǣpst *2nd pers sing pres indic* (158)

slēpon *pl pret indic* (139)

slæpern *neut noun*: dormitory (159)

slǣpst: see **slǣpan**

slecg *fem noun*: sledge hammer

slecgea *gen pl* (124)

slege *masc noun*: blow; *dat sing* (75)

slēpon: see **slǣpan**

smēagan *wk verb*: to deliberate, examine

smēagst *2nd pers sing pres indic* (137)

smiþ *masc noun*: smith, blacksmith (123)

smiþas *acc pl* (116)

smiþþe *fem noun*: smithy (building where a blacksmith works)

smiþþan *dat sing* (124)

sōþ *neut noun*: truth (77, 124)
    sōþlīċe *adv*: truly (110)
spǣċ: see **sp(r)ǣċ**
specst: see **sprecan**
spēdiġ *adj*: wealthy, rich (157)
sp(r)ǣċ *fem noun*: conversation (3, 128)
    sprǣċe *dat sing* (129)
    forþtyhst sprǣċe speak (129)
    sprǣcum *dat pl* (134)
sprecan *str verb*: to speak (1, 2, 3, 7)
    sprec *imper sing* (129, 137)
    sprecaþ *pl pres indic* (1)
    spreċende *pres part* (134)
    sprycst, specst *2nd pers sing pres indic* (6, 126, 129)
spurleþer *neut noun*: spur-strap
    spurleþera *acc pl* (104)
spyrte *fem noun*: basket, eel basket
    spyrtan *acc sing* (57)
standan *str verb*: to stand
    standaþ *imper pl* (162)
    stande *1st pers sing pres indic* (19, 21)
    standende *pres part* (45)
stearc *adj*: hard, rough (11)
stenc *masc noun*: stench, smell
    stence *dat sing* (134)
stiria *masc noun*: sturgeon
    stirian *acc pl* (69)
stīþlīċe *adv*: sternly, forcibly (161)
stōw *fem noun*: place
    stōwe *dat sing* (31, 162)
ġestrangian *wk verb*: to strengthen
    ġestrangie *1st pers sing pres indic* (110)
ġestrēon *neut noun*: profit, gain, property; *acc sing* (100)
stunte *adj*: foolish (131)
sūlh *fem noun*: plow
    sȳl *dat sing* (11)
sum *indef pron and adj*: a certain; certain, some; one, a (100, 110)
    sum(m)e *nom pl* (9)
    sumne *acc sing masc* (14, 70)

sumor *masc noun*: summer (91)
    sumera *dat sing* (90)
sungon: see **singan**
sunnandæġ *masc noun*: Sunday (3)
sunu *masc noun*: son
    sunu *acc sing* (100)
swā *adv and conj*: so, to that extent, such a (11, etc.)
    swā swā: just as (120, 134, 153)
    swā hwæt swā: whatever (49, 57)
    swā hwæðer ... swā ... swā ...: whichever ... whether ... or (127)
    swa wylce swa: whatsoever (65)
swæcc *masc noun*: taste, flavour
    swæcce *dat sing* (108)
swǣs *adj*: sweet, agreeable
    swǣsum *dat pl* (134)
swefel *masc noun*: sulphur (98)
swēġincg *fem noun*: sound, clang, roar
    swēġincga *acc pl* (124)
swelġere *masc noun*: swallower, glutton (151)
swift *adj*: fast, swift
    swiftne *acc sing masc* (85)
    swiftum *dat pl* (35)
swilċe: see **swylċe**
swingell *fem noun*: blow of a rod or whip
    swincgla *acc pl*
swīþe, swȳþe *adv*: very, exceedingly (46, 150)
    swȳþost *adv compar*: most, most often (36)
swyftlēre *masc noun*: slipper
    swytflēras *acc pl* (104)
swylċe, swilċe *adv*: likewise (9, 13, 75, 92)
swylċe *pron*: such
    swylċes *gen sing* (69)
swymman *wk verb*: to swim
    swymmaþ *pl pres indic* (65)
swȳþost: see **swīþe**
syfernyss *fem noun*: moderation
    syfernysse *dat sing* (153)
sȳl: see **sūlh**

syla *masc noun*: plowman
    sylan *dat sing* (123)
sylf *pron*: self
    sylfe *nom/acc pl* (88, 113, 162)
    sylfne *acc sing masc* (127, 135)
ġesyllan *str verb*: to sell, give (63, 99)
    sylle, syle *imper sing* (84, 86); *1st pers sing pres indic* (49, 85, 127)
    sylst *2nd pers sing pres indic* (85, 124)
    sylþ *3rd pers sing pres indic* (50, 51, 124)
symble *adv*: always (127)
synn *fem noun*: sin
    synnum *dat pl* (162)
syþþan *adv*: then, after that (139)

tǣċan *wk verb*: to teach
    tǣċe *2nd pers sing pres subj* (1)
temian/teman *str verb*: to tame (82, 83)
    ġetemedon/ġetemodon *past part* (89, 91)
    temiġe *1st pers sing pres* (88)
tīd *fem noun*: time, occasion
    tīda times; (services at the) canonical hours (7)
ġetihtan *wk verb*: to induce, egg on
    ġetihte *1st pers sing pres indic* (31)
tīma *masc noun*: time (141)
tin *neut noun*: tin; *acc sing* (98)
tō *prep with dat*: to (11, 31, 45, 59, 67, 73, 110, 113, 139, 160, 162)
    tō *adv*: too (110)
tōdæġ *adv*: today (38, 138, 142)
tōforan *prep with dat*: before, in front of (150)
tōġēanes *adv*: opposite; in the way (45)
tōġehyhte: see **tōġeycan**
tōġelædan *wk verb*: to bring, transport
    tōġelæde *1st pers sing pres* (96)
tōġenȳdan *wk verb*: to force, compel
    tōġenȳdd *past part* (5)
tōġeycan *wk verb*: to add
    tōġehyhte *past part* (120)
tōspecan *str verb*: to address, speak to
    tōspycst *3rd pers sing pres indic* (115)
towurpon *str verb*: to dismiss, stop (127)

trēowwyrhta *masc noun*: carpenter (125, 126)
      trēowwyrhtan *acc sing* (116)
treppe *fem noun*: trap
      treppum *dat pl* traps (79)
ġetrȳwe *adj*: true, faithful (19)
twēġen *num*: two (41)
tweowa *adv*: twice (19)
tȳddrian *wk verb*: to produce, bring forth
      tȳddriende *pres part* (134)

þā: see **se**
þā þā *conj*: when (139)
þǣm, þǣne: see **se**
þænne: see **þonne, se**
þǣr *adv*: there, where (45, 99, 100, 127)
þǣrtō *adv*: in addition (19)
þǣs: see **þes**
þæt *conj*: that (1, 11, etc.)
þæt: see **se**
þām: see **se**
þancung *fem noun*: thanks
      þancunge *dat sing* (149)
þanon *adv*: from that, from which (76, 100)
þās: see **þes**
þe *rel pron*: who, which (13, etc.)
þē: see **þū**
þē lustlicor *adv phrase*: so much the more willingly (51)
þeah *conj, adv*: yet; though (76)
ġeþeaht *neut noun*: counsel, advice (127)
ġeþeahta *masc noun*: counsellor
      ġeþeahtan *acc sing* (117)
      ġeþeahtend *masc noun* (124, 127)
      ġeþeahtynde *dat sing* (118)
þēahhwæþere *adv*: nevertheless, moreover (7, 114, 137)
þearle *adv*: hard, very, very much, excessively (11, 90, 102, 106, 115, 129)
þēawlīċe *adv*: obediently (162)
þencan *str verb*: to think
      þencende *pres part* (134)
þēof *masc noun*: thief
      þēofum *dat pl* (21)

þēowdōm *masc noun*: service (120)
þes *dem pron*: this, these
    paes *nom sing masc* (22)
    þās *acc pl* (119, 127)
    þēos *nom sing fem* (128)
    þis *nom sing neut* (127)
    þisse *dat sing fem* (139)
    þisum *dat sing* (96, 127, 139)
    þās þīne ġefēran these companions of yours (8)
þīn, þīnne, þīne, þīnre, þīnum: see þū
þingc, þing *neut noun*: thing (24, 131)
    þinga *gen pl* (96)
    þingc, þincg, þinc *acc pl* (73, 96, 97, 99, 113, 120, 129, 139, 149, 150)
    þinge *dat sing* (111)
þis, þisse, þisum: see þes
þolian *wk verb*: to suffer
    þolie *1st pers sing pres* (96)
þone: see se
þonne, þænne *conj*: when, then; than (5, 21, 73, 100, 114, 124, 125, 126, 137, 141, 150, 162)
þræl *masc noun*: thrall, slave
    þrǣlas *nom pl* (114)
ġeþristian *wk verb*: to dare
    ġeþristġe: *1st pers sing pres* (77)
þrȳste *adj*: daring (46)
þū *pers pron 2nd pers sing*: thou, you (*sing*) (1, 6, 10, etc.)
    þē *acc/dat sing* (1, 5, 6, 50, etc.)
    þīn *gen* (10, 105, 109)
    þīne *nom/acc pl masc/neut* (8, 60, 87, 99, 144)
    þīnne *acc sing masc* (30)
    þīnre *dat sing fem* (48, 124)
    þīnum *dat sing/pl masc* (22, 54)
ġeþuht: see ġeþyncan
þurh *prep with acc*: through, by, by means of (110)
þurhbrūcan *wk verb with dat*: to enjoy to the full
    þurhbrȳcð *3rd pers sing pres indic* (108)
þurhwerod *adj*: very sweet
    þurhwerodum *dat pl* (108)
þus *adv*: thus (114)

þūsenthīwe *adj*: thousand-coloured, thousand-formed (i.e., multiplicitous,
    shifty) (134)
ġeðwǣrian *wk verb*: to agree (127)
ġeþwǣrnyss *fem noun*: peace, agreement (127)
þȳ lǣs *conj phrase*: lest (19)
þylċ *pron*: such
    þylċes *gen sing* (98)
ġeþyncan *impers verb*: to seem
    is ġeþuht: seems (119, 120, 121)
þyrl *neut noun*: hole (126)
þȳwan *str verb*: to drive
    þȳwende *pres part* (11, 13)

ūhtsang *masc noun*: matins (139)
    ūhtsancge *dat sing* (160)
unclǣne *adj*: unclean; *nom pl masc* (58)
    unclǣnan *acc pl masc* (59)
under *prep with dat*: under (147)
understandan *str verb*: to understand (129)
undertīde *fem noun*: tierce (139)
underþēodan *wk verb*: to subject, addict (to)
    underþēodde *past part nom pl* (134)
unēaþe *adv*: not easily, hardly (96)
unforscēawodlīce *adv*: unawares, unexpectedly (31)
unġelǣrede *adj*: unlearned (1)
unscennan *wk verb*: unyoke
    unscenþ *3rd pers sing pres indic* (21)
ūran, ūre, ūs: see wē
ūt *adv*: out (11, 15, 59, 112, 162)
uton *verb pl pres subj of* witan: let us (127)
ūtwyrpan *str verb*: to throw away
    ūtwyrpe *1st pers pres* (59)

wacian *wk verb*: to wake, remain awake
    waciende *pres part* (21)
ġewǣmodlīċe *adv*: corruptly (1)
wǣre: see bēon
wǣrlīċe *adv*: warily, circumspectly (143)
wæs: see bēon

wæter *neut noun*: water (131, 155)
    wætere *dat sing* (65)
wæterian *wk verb*: to water; bring water to (15)
    ġewæterode *past part* (21)
wāt: see **witan**
waxġeorn *adj*: eager to grow, greedy (150)
wē *per pron 1st pers pl nom*: we (1, etc.)
    ūran *poss adj dat pl* (137)
    ūre *gen* (118, 129, 137, 145)
    ūrum *poss adj dat pl; dat neut sing* (127, 129)
    ūs *dat* (5, etc.)
wefod *masc noun*: altar
    wefodum *dat pl* (162)
wel *adv*: well (21, 51, 110, 129, 134)
weliġ *adj*: rich
    weliġum *dat pl* (94)
weorc, weork *neut noun*: work, labour (10)
    weorkes *gen sing* (6)
ġeweorc *neut noun*: work
    ġeweorce *dat sing* (123)
wer *masc noun*: man
    wera *gen pl* (110)
wīf *neut noun*: wife (100)
wīkian *wk verb*: to dwell (124)
wildēor *neut noun*: wild animal
    wildēor *nom/acc pl* (31, 35, 36, 47)
willan *anom verb*: to want to (do something), wish, desire
    wille, wylle *1st pers sing pres indic* (100); *pl pres preposed* (2, 4,
       132, 134, 136, 140)
    wolde *1st pers sing pret subj* (7)
    wyllaþ *3rd pers pl pres indic* (133, 137)
    wylt/wilt *3rd pers sing pret indic/subj* (70, 85, 99)
wīn *neut noun*: wine; *acc sing* (98, 156, 157)
winewincle *fem noun*: periwinkle
    winewinclan *acc pl* (69)
winter *masc noun*: winter (11)
    wintra *dat sing* (88)
wīs *adj*: wise (135)
    wīse *nom pl* (133, 135, 137)

wīsne *acc sing masc* (117)

wīsa *masc noun*: wise man (119)

wīsra *gen pl* (157)

wīsdōm *masc noun*: wisdom

wīsdōme *dat sing* (134)

wīse *fem noun*: way

wīsan *gen pl*: ways (79)

ġewislīċe *adv*: certainly (118)

wissian *wk verb*: to guide, instruct

wissod *past part* (118)

witan *str verb*: to know

wāt *3rd pers sing pres indic* (145)

witaþ *3rd pers pl pres indic* (131)

witodlīċe *adv*: truly, verily (102, 124)

witun *pl pres indic* (5)

wiþinnan *adv*: within (134)

wlætta *masc noun*: a nauseating substance

wlættan *dat sing* (110)

wolde: see willan

word *neut noun*: word

wordum *dat pl* (134)

woruldcræft *masc noun*: secular occupation

woruldcræftas *acc pl* (121)

wudu *masc noun*: wood

wuda *dat sing* (88)

wudum *dat pl* (47)

wulf *masc noun*: wolf

wulfas *nom pl* (19)

ġewuna *masc noun*: custom, practice, habit

ġewunon *dat pl* (137)

wunian *wk verb*: to dwell, live

wuniaþ *3rd pers pl pres indic* (47)

wylle, wyllaþ, wylt: see willan

wynsume *adj*: winsome, gracious, joyful (162)

wyrcan *wk verb*: to do, make

wyrce *1st pers sing pres indic* (104, 125)

wyrcst *2nd pers sing pres indic* (20, 101)

wyrhta *masc noun*: worker

wyrhtan *nom pl* (127)

wyrhtum *dat pl* (127)

wyrpan *str verb*: to throw
       wyrpe *1st pers sing pres* (57)
wyrt *fem noun*: vegetable
         wyrtum *dat pl* (108)
         wyrta *acc pl* (112, 149)
wyrtġemangc *neut noun*: mixture of spices; *acc pl* (98)
ġewyslīċe *adv*: certainly, indeed, of course (15)

yfel *neut noun*: evil
       yfele *dat sing* (137)
yfele *adv*: evilly (134)
yld *fem noun:* age (137)
ylpesbān *neut noun*: ivory (98)
yppan *wk verb*: to reveal, betray (145)
yrþlincg, yrþlingc, yrþling *masc noun*: a farmer, plowman (10, 122, 124)
         yrþlincgas *nom pl* (9)
         yrþlincge *dat sing* (21, 124, 127)
ytst: see **etan**

Select Bibliography

◆

This bibliography lists only a few of the resources that a student might consult for additional information about the grammar of Old English and about the texts used in *A Gentle Introduction*. Some of the items listed here are not suitable for beginners. If you are studying Old English in a course and have a specific question, your first point of inquiry in seeking additional resources should always be your teacher.

Grammar

Brunner, Karl. *Altenglische Grammatik nach der Angelsächsischen Grammatik von Eduard Sievers*. 3rd edition. Tübingen: Niemeyer, 1965. [Sievers-Brunner]

Unfortunately only available in German, but more comprehensive than Campbell.

Campbell, A. *Old English Grammar*. Oxford: Clarendon, 1959.

The standard English-language grammar.

Hogg, Richard. *A Grammar of Old English: Phonology*. Oxford: Blackwell, 1992.
Hogg, Richard, and R.D. Fulk. *A Grammar of Old English, Volume II: Morphology*. Oxford: Wiley-Blackwell, 2010.

Although somewhat massive even for most keen graduate students, this new grammar supersedes both Campbell and Sievers-Brunner.

Mitchell, Bruce. *Old English Syntax*. 2 vols. Oxford: Clarendon, 1985.

> A thorough and comprehensive study of word order; case use; sentence, phrase, and clause structure; and other syntactic matters.

Mitchell, Bruce, and Fred C. Robinson. *A Guide to Old English*. 7th ed. Oxford: Blackwell, 2007.

> This standard textbook contains a very full account of Old English grammar. Copies of earlier editions are widely available on the used book market.

Texts

Bately, Janet, and Anton Englert, eds. *Ohthere's Voyages: A Late 9th-Century Account of Voyages along the Coasts of Norway and Denmark and Its Cultural Context*. Roskilde, Denmark: Viking Ship Museum, 2007.

> Provides facsimiles of the manuscripts, text, translation and notes, and a variety of articles illuminating aspects of Ohthere and his voyage.

Crawford, S.J., ed. *The Old English Version of the Heptateuch*. Early English Text Society. Oxford: Oxford UP, 1922.

Liuzza, R.M., ed. *The Old English Version of the Gospels*. 2 vols. Early English Text Society. Oxford: Oxford UP, 1994, 2003.

> Together, these two editions provide the extant Old English translations of substantial portions of the Old and New Testaments.

Garmonsway, G.N. *Ælfric's Colloquy*. 2nd ed. London: Methuen, 1947.

> The standard edition of the *Colloquy*, with Old English and Latin texts, full glossary, and notes.

Index

◆

Abraham and Isaac (Genesis 22:1-19), 101–15
accusative case, 46–47, 60–61, 63
adjectives
  comparison of, 80
  declensions of, 78–80
  as nouns, 80–81
  participles, 53–54
  parts of speech, 17
  possessive adjectives, 67–68
  See also demonstratives
adverbs, 17, 62–63
Ælfric, 153–54
Aelfric's Colloquy, 151–98
Alfred the Great (king), 129
alliteration, 92–93, 94–95
alphabet, 23
Anglo-Saxon Chronicle, 39–40
apposition, 98–99
articles, 15–16

bearn (child), 32, 36, 59
bēon (to be), 42–44, 90–91
Beowulf, 96
Bible, 54–56, 101–15, 117–25
Birth of Jesus (Luke 2: 1-21), 54–56, 117–25
biscop (bishop), 31
brōðor (brother), 74

brūcan (to enjoy, use, profit from), 61
brȳd (bride), 32, 37, 59
burg, burh (city, town, castle), 72–73

"Caedmon's Hymn," 92–93, 98
cases
  accusative case, 46–47, 60–61, 63
  adverbial use of, 62–63
  case harmony, 33
  dative case, 46–47, 60, 62
  general case (modern English), 20
  genitive case, 30, 38–39, 60, 63
  instrumental case, 62
  nominative case, 30, 38
  objective case (modern English), 21
  poetic use of, 96
  possessive case (modern English), 20
  prepositions, 60–61
  subjective case (modern English), 21
  verbs, 61–62
clauses, 18
commands, 51–52

comparative form (adjectives), 80
compound nouns, 95
compound verbs, 16, 53–54
conjecture, 52
conjugation (of verbs)
    classes of verbs, 21
        irregular verbs, 21
        regular verbs, 21
        strong verbs, 21, 45, 65–66
        weak verbs, 45, 71–72
    See also verbs
conjugation tables
    about, 42–43
    bēon (to be), 42–44, 90–91
    ġiefan (to give), 45
    habban (to have), 44, 90–91
    helpan (to help), 65–66
    lufian (to love), 45, 50–51
conjunctions
    coordinating conjunctions, 18
    correlating conjunctions, 88
    part of speech, 18
consonant sounds, 24–26
cyning (king), 30, 33, 47, 58

dative case, 46–47, 60, 62
declensions, 30
    See also nouns; paradigm tables
definite article, 15–16
demonstrative pronouns. See
    demonstratives
demonstratives
    feminine and neuter, 36–37
    masculine **se**-demonstrative, 33,
        37–38
    þes (this, these), 81–82
    See also adjectives
deprivation, 62
diphthongs, 28
direct object, 19–20, 46
dohtor (daughter), 74

ēage (eye), 72

fæder (father), 74
family terms, 73–75
feminine demonstratives, 36–37
feminine nouns
    family terms, 74
        grammatical gender, 31–32
        strong feminine nouns, 32–33,
        37
        vowel changes, 72–73
        weak feminine nouns, 72
first person, 16

gender. See grammatical gender
general case (modern English), 20
Genesis, 101–15
genitive case
    in paradigm tables, 30
    plural genitive, 39
    prepositions, 60
    time expressions, 63
    uses of, 38–39
genitive pronouns, 67–68
ġiefan (to give), 45
ġiefu (gift), 59–60
grammatical gender, 31–32
habban (to have), 44, 90–91
hearpe (harp), 72
helpan (to help), 65–66
hunta (hunter), 71

imperative mood, 16, 51–52
indefinite article, 15–16
indefinite pronouns, 15
indicative mood, 16, 51–52
indirect object, 19–20, 46
infinitives, 52–53
inflections, 20, 53
    See also conjugation (of verbs)
instrumental case, 62

interrogative pronouns, 15, 82–83
irregular verbs, 21

Jesus (birth of), 54–56, 117–25

linking verbs, 19
Luke (book of), 54–56, 117–25

main clause, 18
mann (man, person), 72–73
masculine nouns
 family terms, 74–75
 grammatical gender, 31–32
 strong masculine nouns,
  46–47, 58
 vowel changes, 72–73
 weak masculine nouns, 71
masculine **se**-demonstrative, 33,
 37–38
metre (Old English poetry), 92–94
mīn, 69
mōdor (mother), 74
mood, 16, 51–52, 89–90

neuter demonstratives, 36–37
neuter nouns
 grammatical gender, 31–32
 strong neuter nouns, 32–33, 59
nominative case, 30, 38
noun paradigms. *See* paradigm
 tables
noun phrases
 apposition, 98–99
 parts of speech, 14–15
 se-demonstrative, 37–38
 word order in, 85–87
 See also subject
nouns
 adjectives as, 80–81
  compound nouns, 95
  family terms, 73–75

inflections, 20
 numerals, 75–76
 parts of speech, 14–15
 poetry, 97
 prepositions, 60–61
 strong nouns, 32–33, 37,
  46–47, 58
 vowel changes in, 72–73
 weak nouns, 71–72
 See also cases; grammatical
  gender; pronouns; subject
numerals, 75–76

objective case (modern English), 21
objects
 direct object, 19–20, 46
 indirect object, 19–20, 46
 prepositions, 17, 60–61
 transitive verbs, 46–47
 verbs, 19–20, 61–62
Ohthere (voyage of), 47–48,
 127–49
Orosius, Paulus, 47, 129

paradigm tables (by noun type)
 about, 30
 adjectives, 79
 family terms, 73–75
 interrogative pronouns, 82–83
 masculine demonstrative, 33
 pronouns, 67–68
 strong feminine nouns, 32, 37,
  59–60
 strong masculine nouns,
  30–31, 33, 46–47, 58
 strong neuter nouns, 32, 36,
  59
 vowel changing nouns, 72–73
 weak feminine noun, 72
 weak masculine noun, 71
 weak neuter noun, 72

paradigm tables (specific nouns)
  bearn (child), 32, 36, 59
  biscop (bishop), 31
  brōðor (brother), 74
  brȳd (bride), 32, 37, 59
  burg, burh (city, town, castle),
    72–73
  cyning (king), 30, 33, 47, 58
  dohtor (daughter), 74
  ēage (eye), 72
  fæder (father), 74
  ġiefu (gift), 59–60
  hearpe (harp), 72
  hunta (hunter), 71
  mann (man, person), 72–73
  mōdor (mother), 74
  scip (ship), 59
  stān (stone), 30
  sunu (son), 75
  sweostor, swustor, swostor
    (sister), 74
participles, 53–54
parts of a sentence. *See* sentences
parts of speech
  adjectives, 17
    adverbs, 17
    articles, 15–16
    conjunctions, 18
    nouns, 14–15
    overview of, 18
    prepositions, 17
    pronouns, 15
    verbs, 16
personal pronouns. *See* pronouns
phrases, 18
plural genitive, 39
poetry
  metre of, 92–94
    poetic diction, 94–96
    poetic style, 98–99
    syntax of, 96–97

possessive adjectives, 67–68
possessive case (modern English),
  20
predicate, 16, 18–19
prepositions
  cases, 60–61
    parts of speech, 17
    prepositional phrases, 17
pronouns
  cases, 21
    declension of, 67–68
    genitive pronouns, 67–68
    indefinite pronouns, 15
    interrogative pronouns, 15,
    82–83
  mīn, 69
  part of speech, 15
  poetry, 97
  relative pronouns, 15
  verb tables, 43
  See also nouns; subject
pronouns (demonstrative). *See*
  demonstratives
pronunciation
  consonant sounds, 24–26
    diphthongs, 28
    how to study, 24
    knowledge of, 23–24
    nouns, 72–73
    strong verbs, 66–67
    vowel sounds, 27–29

questions. *See* interrogative pronouns

regular verbs (modern English), 21,
  45
relative pronouns, 15
rhythmical patterns, 93–94

scip (ship), 59

second person, 16
sentences
    predicate, 16, 18–19
    subject, 18–19
    verbs and objects, 19–20
    word order, 87–89
short vowels, 27
Sievers, Eduard, 93–94
Sievers' Five Types, 93–94
simple verbs, 16
sound changes.
    See pronunciation
speech (parts of). *See* parts of
    speech
stān (stone), 30
Story of Ohthere, 47–48, 127–49
strong declensions of adjectives,
    78–80
strong nouns, 32–33
    feminine nouns, 59–60
    masculine nouns, 46–47, 58
    neuter nouns, 59
strong verbs
    conjugation of, 21, 45, 65–66
    pronunciation, 66–67
subject
    sentence structure, 18–19
    subject complement, 19
    verbs, 16
    See also noun phrases; nouns;
        pronouns
subjective case (modern English),
    21
subjunctive mood, 51–52, 89–91
subordinate clauses, 18
subordinating conjunctions, 18
sunu (son), 75
superlative form (of adjectives),
    80
sweostor, swustor, swostor (sister),
    74

tense
    participles, 53–54
    verbs, 16
þes (this, these), 81–82
third person, 16
time expressions, 63
transitive verbs, 19, 46–47

verb tables. *See* conjugation tables
verbs
    cases, 61–62
    compound verbs, 16, 53–54
    deprivation, 62
    infinitives, 52–53
    inflections, 20
    linking verbs, 19
    mood, 16, 51–52, 89–91
    objects, 19–20
    participles, 53–54
    parts of speech, 16
    regular verbs, 45
    simple verbs, 16
    strong verbs, 45, 65–67
    subjects, 16
    tense, 16
    transitive verbs, 19, 46–47
    weak verbs, 50–51
    See also conjugation (of
        verbs)
vowels
    diphthongs, 28
    Great Vowel Shift, 27
    long vowels, 27–28
    nouns, 72–73
    pronunciation, 27–29
    short vowels, 27
    strong verbs, 66–67

weak adjectives, 78–80
weak nouns, 71–72
    feminine nouns, 72

masculine nouns, 71
neuter nouns, 72
weak verbs, 45, 50–51
web site addresses, 12
wishes, 52
word order
correlating conjunctions, 88
noun phrases, 85–87

overview, 34
poetic, 96–97
prepositions, 61
sentences, 87–89